A PROPOSAL
Key to an Effective Foreign Policy

A PROPOSAL

HARPER & BROTHERS   NEW YORK

Key to an Effective Foreign Policy

by MAX F. MILLIKAN

Professor of Economics
Massachusetts Institute of Technology

and W. W. ROSTOW

Professor of Economic History
Massachusetts Institute of Technology

With the collaboration of P. N. ROSENSTEIN-RODAN
and others at the Center for International Studies
Massachusetts Institute of Technology

CONTENTS

v

PREFACE

This book has a number of roots. In 1952 the Center for International Studies at M.I.T. launched a major program of research into the economic, social, and political processes involved in the efforts most of the so-called underdeveloped countries are making to raise their living standards. The ultimate purpose of most of the studies the Center undertakes is to throw light on crucial long-range policy problems confronting the United States, in this instance: What role can and should the United States play in promoting economic growth abroad? Our researches, which the Ford Foundation and the Rockefeller Foundation have generously financed, were designed to include intensive studies on a number of countries, notably India, Indonesia, and Italy.

Our plan envisaged a schedule stretching over a number of years, starting with a period of research planning followed by field work in each of the three countries selected for intensive study and ending with a year or two of analysis and synthesis of our results. We planned to defer consideration of the policy issues on which our work was designed to throw light until 1957-58, after the background studies had been completed. These policy issues were, however, of such compelling current interest that we began to receive requests for our policy views from a number of quarters almost as soon as the research program had been launched. We resisted these pressures until we felt that our work had progressed far enough to give us some confidence in the validity of a few key propositions.

All of the senior members of the staff of the Center's economic development research program had had experience with development problems before starting on the current research effort. One of the present authors, W. W. Rostow, had for years devoted his efforts as an economic historian to the study of the economic growth of the presently industrialized countries. He had worked with the Economic Commission for Europe in Geneva during the European recovery period and had also devoted three years of research to the relation between economic and political change in studies of the evolution of Soviet Russia and Communist China undertaken for the Center. The other author, M. F. Millikan, had worked as an economist on the measurement of national income and product and the determinants of changes in these magnitudes and had directed a research program on the Soviet economy. He had been on the staffs of the Harriman and Herter Committees on the Marshall Plan and had assisted Gordon Gray in preparing his Report to the President on Foreign Economic Policies. Other members of the Center staff such as P. N. Rosenstein-Rodan, Everett Hagen, Benjamin Higgins, and Wilfred Malenbaum had held positions in the International

Bank and the economic offices of the U.S. State Department, or as advisors to the governments of such underdeveloped countries as Burma, Indonesia, and Libya. Thus we felt that our collective experience was sufficient to justify us in responding to requests for our ideas on policy before all the returns from our current program were in.

In 1954, shortly after he resigned from his position as Special Assistant to the President for International Affairs, Mr. C. D. Jackson took the initiative for calling together a group of individuals, mainly from private life but including some government officials, to discuss informally ways in which the United States might play a more constructive and more positive role in building a stable world, a role which would complement our primarily military efforts to insure security against aggression. After participating in the resulting discussion, the present authors were asked to prepare a paper setting forth their views on what part U.S. policy with respect to the promotion of economic growth abroad might play in such a constructive foreign policy. The paper prepared in response to that wholly unofficial request was the first draft of the present book. The Center, as time went on, received numerous requests for this paper from persons who had seen the first draft. While the 1956 Foreign Aid Bill was under consideration, a revised draft was circulated to interested members of Congress and of the Administration and to private citizens of both major political parties. Our views underwent some modification as a result both of a great many helpful comments made on that draft, and of information developed by our research program. In view of the re-examination of U.S. economic assistance programs undertaken by both the Congress and the Executive Branch of the U.S. Government in the summer of 1956, we concluded that the time had come to make our analysis more widely available for such use as it might be to the increasing numbers of people both here and abroad concerned with this problem.

While the authors are confident of the validity of the main lines of the argument set forth here, this book is still an interim report. Its conclusions will be revised, amplified, and we hope more fully documented as our research proceeds. The book is in a very real sense a collective effort. While the two of us take full responsibility for the views expressed, we have depended at many points on other Center staff members who have contributed many of the ideas in the book. We have drawn particularly heavily on the wisdom and experience of our colleague, Paul Rosenstein-Rodan, former Research Director of the International Bank, who in addition to suggesting a number of the central concepts has reviewed several drafts of the manuscript in detail.

We would like also to record our indebtedness not only to the other senior members of the Center's economic development staff, Messrs. Hagen, Higgins, and Malenbaum, but also to Francis Bator, George Baldwin, Harold Isaacs, and Ithiel Pool. Such stylistic clarity as the book possesses is due in large measure to the careful editing of Richard Hatch and Donald Blackmer. It is impossible to list all the persons outside the Center who have, by their comments on successive drafts, improved both the content and the clarity of exposition. Richard Eckaus and Melville Watkins asssisted in the preparation of the Appendix.

MAX F. MILLIKAN

W. W. ROSTOW

Cambridge, Massachusetts
August 27, 1956

A PROPOSAL
Key to an Effective Foreign Policy

1 THE PURPOSES OF THE PROGRAM

The Thesis

IT IS THE THESIS OF THIS BOOK that a much-expanded long-term program of American participation in the economic development of the under-developed areas can and should be one of the most important means for furthering the purposes of American foreign policy. We believe that such a program is one of the few concrete instruments available to us for achieving the twofold result of: (1) increasing the awareness elsewhere in the world that the goals, aspirations, and values of the American people are in large part the same as those of peoples in other countries; and (2) developing viable, energetic, and confident democratic societies through the Free World. We believe, therefore, that such a program could be a principal and effective instrument in our efforts to produce political, social, and psychological results in the national interest.

The program we propose would require U.S. government expenditure somewhat larger than current spending for economic aid. But the amount of additional money needed would be small compared with what we shall have to spend in emergency efforts either to salvage situations which have been permitted to degenerate, such as South Korea and Indo-China, or to put out additional brushfires if they get started. The total costs of such a program would be insignificant compared with the costs of waging limited wars.

The Foreign Policy Context

We are acutely aware that, insofar as the U.S. national interest is taken as a point of departure, there are fundamental differences of American opinion as to what constitute the principal dangers and opportunities confronting us in our relations with the rest of the world. It is important, therefore, before developing in detail the case for a new economic assistance program for the United States, to outline the foreign policy context into which the program we propose is designed to fit.

There are two priority tasks for U.S. foreign policy.* The first of these is to meet effectively the threat to our security posed by the danger of overt military aggression, a threat now inherent in the present capabilities and possible future intentions of the Communist bloc countries. This

* These general tasks of American foreign policy are considered at greater length in Chapter 13 and related to our proposals.

threat is to be met primarily by maintaining or increasing U.S. military strength and by solidifying alliances with other countries in a position to contribute significantly to that strength. One of the instruments to be used in this effort is economic assistance to countries with important industrial potential, mainly the NATO powers, designed to make that potential militarily more effective.

The second priority task of U.S. foreign policy is to promote the evolution of a world in which threats to our security and, more broadly, to our way of life are less likely to arise. Success in this task would mean the freeing of a large volume of resources from military to more constructive uses. More important, it would mean protecting our society from the pressures inevitably associated with a garrison state, pressures which threaten our most cherished values. It is this task with which this book is mainly concerned.

What does success in this second task require?

Here the most serious differences on foreign policy arise among thoughtful men. Some would emphasize the importance of organizational arrangements for collective security—a better structure for the United Nations; a system of bilateral, multilateral, or world-wide international agreements; institutions to reduce the importance of national sovereignty like European Union, World Federalism, and the like. Some would emphasize ideological considerations —the necessity to counter and expose systems of thought like communism which have a built-in commitment to violence as an instrument of change; the importance of restating systematically and promulgating widely the values of

Western democratic liberalism in a form which would be irresistibly persuasive to peoples everywhere. Some would emphasize the importance of creating social, economic, and political conditions in which violence and protest would lose their appeal because more attractive methods were available for satisfying personal and collective aspirations. Obviously all these approaches and others besides are needed.

Underlying the proposals in this book is the conviction that we have put relatively too much emphasis in recent years on pacts, treaties, negotiation, and international diplomacy and too little on measures to promote the evolution of stable, effective, and democratic societies abroad which can be relied upon not to generate conflict because their own national interests parallel ours and because they are politically healthy and mature. This conviction, in turn, is based upon an estimate of the nature of the forces at work in the world making for change.

The Great Transition

It has become a commonplace that we are in the midst of a great world revolution. For centuries the bulk of the world's population has been politically inert. Outside America and Western Europe, and even in parts of the latter, until recently the pattern of society remained essentially fixed in the mold of low-productivity rural life centered on isolated villages. The possibility of change for most people seemed remote, and political activity was confined to an extremely small elite. Within the past forty years two world wars and a phenomenal increase in the ease and effectiveness of communication have fundamentally altered the perspectives of hundreds of millions of people. Countries with populations aggregating over half a billion have just won their independence and are trying to cope with their new status. The rapidly accelerating spread of literacy, mass communications, and travel, which has only begun, will produce even more unsettling results over the coming years.

This revolution is rapidly exposing previously apathetic peoples to the possibility of change. It is creating in them new aspirations for education, social improvement, and economic development. At the same time, it is breaking down traditional institutions and culture patterns which in the past held their societies together. In short, the world community is becoming both more interdependent and more fluid than it has been at any other time in history, a condition which presents us with both a great danger and a great opportunity.

The Danger to the United States

The danger is that increasing numbers of people will become convinced that their new aspirations can be realized only through violent change and the renunciation of democratic institutions. That danger has no single cause. It is inherent in the revolutionary process. But it is greatly increased by the existence of communism—not because of any authentic attractions in its ideology but because the Communists have recognized their opportunities to exploit the revolution of rising expectations by picturing communism as the road to social opportunity or economic improvement or individual dignity and achievement or national self-respect, whichever fitted a given situation.

Thus, the dangers of instability inherent in the awakening of formerly static peoples would be present even in the absence of the Communist apparatus, as is demonstrated by the existence of trouble spots like Kenya and Morocco— apparently relatively unconnected with Communist subversion. But the danger is, of course, greatly intensified by the focus which both Communist thought and Communist organization give.

The United States has not presented a consistent and persuasive alternative in terms of the democratic process. It is the unpleasant truth that the United States has come to be regarded increasingly in the uncommitted areas of the world as a power at best neurotic and at worst aggressive, preoccupied with military preparations and with a game of international power diplomacy which has no meaning for the newly awakened ordinary citizen. We are no longer identified, as we once were, with the aspirations of people for social and economic improvement or with their Utopian image of a society designed to satisfy those aspirations.

The American Opportunity

The economic development program outlined in the balance of this book is conceived as one of the instruments for carrying out the task of helping create an environment within which American society can thrive. It stands or falls on the acceptance of this task as one of the two top priority objectives of U.S. foreign policy. It cannot be too strongly emphasized that this program is only one of many instruments which must be used in a co-ordinated way if we are to maximize our influence to promote the development of stable, effective, and democratic societies elsewhere in the world. Information policy, military assistance, and conventional diplomacy have jobs to do which are not now being done. Economic policy by itself will not achieve the desired result. And if an economic policy is to contribute to the creation of stable and democratic societies it must be carefully conceived with this end in view. As will be suggested in the next chapter, a development assistance policy narrowly designed to win friends or promote military alliances could easily backfire and produce results actually detrimental to our national interest.

While it is obvious that the political, social, and economic development of foreign areas is a task for the peoples of these areas themselves, and that we alone cannot insure that they will do it well or badly, two considerations suggest that it would be inexcusable for the United States and the other developed nations of the Free World not to exert to the utmost whatever influence they have. In the first place, we have a compelling national interest in promoting a world environment in which we ourselves can live freely, secure from both the menace of hostile states and from the distraction of chaotic ones. In the second place, American society is at its best when we are wrestling with the positive problems of building a better world. Our own continent provided such a challenge throughout the nineteenth century; the problem of reconciling a mature industrial society with the principles of our democracy provided such a challenge in the first half of the twentieth century. As our emergence into national maturity lifts our horizons beyond our own shores, and as we come to agree as a people how to manage democratically our mature capitalist economy, we need the challenge of world development to keep us from the stagnation of smug prosperity.

Our great opportunity lies in the fact that we have developed more successfully than any other nation the social, political, and economic techniques for realizing widespread popular desires for change without either compulsion or social disorganization. Although our techniques must be adapted to local conditions abroad if they are to be effective there, they represent an enormous potential for steering the world's newly aroused human energies in constructive rather than destructive directions.

Moreover, deep in American society, hankering for effective expression, capable of mobilization, is a dedication to the fundamental principles of national independence and human liberty under law. In their largest sense the proposals in this book are designed to give fresh meaning and vitality to the historic American sense of mission—a mission to see the principles of national independence and human liberty extended on the world scene.

2   SOME FALLACIES AND PITFALLS

A PROGRAM ADOPTED FOR THE wrong reasons may well be worse than useless. It is therefore important to examine some current misconceptions as to the purposes of assistance programs.

Are economic assistance programs intended mainly to win friends for the United States? To strengthen the military capabilities of our allies? To induce other countries to follow foreign policies to our liking? To reduce the appeal of communism to the poverty stricken? To benefit the United States economically? To induce healthy internal political development abroad? To raise living standards for humanitarian reasons?

Since much of the hostility toward foreign assistance programs arises from wrong ideas as to their purposes and as to the political and psychological effects that they can be expected to have, it is well to take a look at some of the current misconceptions before proceeding to develop the positive case.

We would note four widely prevalent errors.

Should Aid Bring Us Friends?

The simplest misconception is that assistance extended by us will insure friendship and gratitude and that these in turn will insure behavior in our interest. Anyone familiar with the psychology of the grantor-grantee relationship will not consciously fall into this error. The relationship is a complex and frequently corrosive one. The grantee's sense of dependence often produces feelings of resentment toward the grantor which may worsen rather than improve relations between the two. We must expect that an incidental result of assistance may frequently be the appearance of less rather than more spirit of co-operation and mutual respect even, and perhaps especially, if the assistance is successful in achieving its real objectives. Although this fact is accepted intellectually by most perceptive observers, even those who are clearest about it are often emotionally hurt by evidences of what looks like gross ingratitude. Such an emotional reaction produces a state of mind in which serious mistakes may be made in the design of economic programs; for the measures which can be taken to lessen the hostile reactions to economic assistance are often the precise opposite of those likely to be taken by an official smarting from hurt or spurred by a Congress so "hurt."

Surely, our central objective is not to get people to say

they like us and will join with us. Winning fair-weather friends is not a fundamental objective of U.S. policy. It is therefore essential to conduct aid programs so as to prevent, as far as possible, emotional reactions which might lead to a rejection or interruption of the programs themselves which have the quite different objectives outlined later in this book. Our public role as donor must be minimized, not maximized. The fullest possible credit must be given the recipient for his own contributions. Demands for demonstrations of alliance and agreement must be reduced rather than increased.

In a deeper sense it is, of course, altogether likely that a program requiring that many Americans work side by side with others in a common enterprise of mutual interest will develop human friendship and a sense of national partnership. This was an important long term by-product of the Marshall Plan. But friendship, even of this important kind, is not the primary justification for the effort required of the United States in the program outlined here.

Should Aid Strengthen Foreign Military Capabilities?

A second misconception is that the central purpose of economic aid programs is always to enable the recipient countries to carry a much larger share of the burden of military build-up against Communist armed forces. We believe there is an excellent case for military assistance to allies who, as in Western Europe, have real industrial potential, but that this case has been extended much too uncritically to the less developed areas.

In the first place, the resources of most of the under-developed areas are so limited that even with massive aid the contribution they could make to defense against open military aggression by the Communist nations inevitably would be very small. We must face squarely up to the fact that resistance to determined military aggression by the Soviet bloc powers is a job for the United States with help from the NATO powers of Western Europe, and that any hope that we can create and maintain such a defense cheaply by organizing the manpower masses of Asia is largely illusory.

In the second place, while the underdeveloped countries can help to resist minor aggression and should be able to maintain order internally, weapons and military potential are ineffective without the will to use them. Some countries appear to have this will, others clearly do not. Our efforts to force military assistance on countries which do not want it may actually weaken such will as exists. Such efforts convince them that we are trying to involve them for our own purposes in disputes which they could otherwise stay out of, and they compound the widespread conviction in Asia and elsewhere that U.S. objectives are mainly military and aggressive.

There is a further consideration which suggests that, even in those underdeveloped countries whose governments are willing or eager to expand their military establishments beyond the requirements of internal order, we should proceed only with caution to meet their wishes. A crucial, perhaps decisive, difference between the Communist formula for economic growth and the Free World formula is that the Free World formula offers to all the citizens of a country the hope that their emerging aspirations for economic, social, and political betterment can be at least partly satisfied as the process of development proceeds. The Communists promise this but are unable to make good on their promise precisely because their pattern of development emphasizes the heavy industrial growth important to military power at the expense of the agricultural and light industrial development essential to improved citizen welfare. It is this perversion of economic development to the creation of military power which, in turn, makes necessary many of the instruments of force and repression which characterize Communist states. The collection of grain to supply the food requirements of armies has been used in China, Indo-China, and elsewhere to justify the abandonment of freedoms and the corrosion of the political process at the village level.

Pressing for a disproportionately large military investment by a poor country runs the risk of either preventing the economy from growing or persuading the country's leaders to adopt totalitarian measures to force growth in the face of lack of popular enthusiasm.

Should Aid Guarantee Reliance on Private Enterprise?

The expectation that American aid programs can and should be used to halt or reverse the trend toward "socialism" present in many underdeveloped areas may find expression in either of two kinds of policy attitudes.

Some argue that we should use offers of assistance to force countries to abandon proposed government enterprises and to establish conditions favorable to the maximum degree of domestic and foreign private investment. These persons believe that the attractions of economic assistance are great enough to induce countries to abandon their already adopted avowedly socialist goals and reorient their whole philosophy of the relation between the state and the economy to that which prevailed in nineteenth-century America. The second group believe that, although a country may adopt any philosophy it likes, no U.S. resources should be devoted to assisting governments which have socialist objectives. If other nations go all out for a free private enterprise system, we will provide capital to support their economic growth; if they adopt a different view, as India and Burma have done, for example, we shall not interfere—but we shall let them go their way without our help.

The authors believe that both of these attitudes are likely to frustrate what we conceive to be the basic purposes of economic assistance. We agree with those who hold a private market system with opportunity and incentive for individual enterprise will in the long run promote self-sustaining growth better than a highly bureaucratized system dominated by central government. But we believe that we shall ultimately promote reliance on private incentives more effectively by not insisting on any particular economic philosophy as a condition of aid than by attaching private enterprise strings. In many situations a favorable environment for private investment can be established only after a period of rather heavy capital formation under government auspices. This is what happened in Japan in the decade after 1868. More recently, the whole set of measures instituted by the Indian government in the period starting in 1951 have, by 1956, created an environment in which Indian private enterprise is undergoing rapid growth.

Thus we believe on the one hand that crude attempts to force a free private enterprise philosophy on recipient countries as an explicit or implicit condition for aid are almost certain to be self-defeating; on the other hand we believe there are good reasons for expecting countries now avowedly socialist but determinedly democratic to move toward greater reliance on private enterprise as their development proceeds. Taking this attitude, our national policy should reflect a well-grounded confidence that, in the light of the experiences of the postwar decade, socialists all over the world have abandoned or are in the process of abandoning their old doctrinaire faith in nationalization as a cure-all.

Part of the reason for this paradox lies in the meanings attached to key words. Among intellectuals in many Asian countries, the term "socialism" has become synonymous with values to which we also are dedicated: equality of opportunity, the public welfare as the test of economic performance, equitable distribution of income, protection of the individual against risks over which he has no control, acceptance by each citizen of his social responsibilities, and so on. On the other hand, in these same countries, the term "capitalism" has assumed a meaning largely derived from Marxist literature. To many Asians, literate and illiterate alike, capitalism implies exploitation of the less fortunate, pursuit of selfish private gain with no regard for public welfare, huge concentration of economic power in a few irresponsible hands, and wasteful dog-eat-dog competition ruthlessly destroying the weak or idealistic. Such stereotypes blind both Americans and Asians to the fact that there is a large body of values both groups share. Such stereotypes often misrepresent the actual organization of economic activity. In the avowedly "capitalist" United States the government directly determines some 20 per cent of the output of the economy, while in avowedly "socialist" India government determines only about 8 per cent.

But whatever the actual character of the economies, the stereotypes exist; and they are deeply rooted. To connect our assistance with a frontal attack on socialist ideology will result in all probability in a refusal of aid and a vigorous reassertion of socialist principles. Technical assistance programs which provide opportunities for us to demonstrate how we in fact approach concrete economic problems can over time have a very helpful influence in correcting these false images of our economic system. They can also correct false images in the United States of what Asian and Anglo-Scandinavian "socialism" stands for.

Apart from these semantic questions, there is the problem of the degree to which substantial state promotion is essential for a rapid transition from stagnation to economic growth. Many of the kinds of investment required are inherently of a public character. Roads, harbors, communication and transportation facilities, sanitation, and community services of all kinds often must be developed ahead of the market demand for them. Even in the United States it was Federal, state, and local government units rather than private enterprise which provided these overheads in the nineteenth century. Moreover, many types of investment which in advanced economies are undertaken privately may have to be launched initially by public bodies in the underdeveloped economies. The risks of many kinds of industrial investment in a preindustrial economy are not of a sort private capital can be expected to bear. In economies where no substantial body of enterprising private businessmen has yet been developed, adequate managerial and administrative talent may be very scarce in the private sector but relatively abundant in a civil service which has traditionally recruited the best talent in the society. Where the institutions for mobilizing private capital are rudimentary or nonexistent, only government may be able to muster the resources for major investment. For these and other reasons, then, there are situations in which development must already be firmly under way before it is reasonable to expect private investment to take primary initiative for pushing it forward. In such situations, insisting that investment must be wholly or largely privately administered from the start may prevent the preconditions for private investment from being established.

These conclusions will discourage those who cling to the belief that in any society any extension of government activity beyond minimal caretaker functions carries with it

the gravest threats to political liberty and individual freedom. The authors do not share that belief. We believe that
the crucial prerequisites for a free society are a dedication
to voluntary rather than compulsory methods, a widespread
dispersion throughout the citizenry of power over crucial
decisions, the presence of genuine freedom of debate and
dissent, and a legal framework which insures against the
arbitrary use of the instruments of force. In addition, we
believe that sustained economic growth in a democratic
society probably requires a pattern of incentives which encourages maximum participation in economic decision-
making by all the alert and imaginative elements in the
society. A largely private business system such as ours in the
United States is one way of achieving this participation.
Other ways may be better adapted to the preconceptions
and culture patterns of other societies, at least in the early
stages. The hope that we can, through aid programs, force
upon these other societies the precise type of economic institution we prefer is bound to lead to disappointment and
frustration.

The other side of the coin is the reasonable hope that, as
societies achieve some success in spreading the benefits
of economic growth among their peoples, as education becomes universal, as markets expand, as a managerial class is
established, as the prerequisite social overheads of transport,
communication, power, and community facilities are established, as savings grow large enough to support private
ventures, there will be increasing scope for private economic
activity whatever the name attached to the economic

philosophy. This is particularly likely if the choice between public and private enterprise is, in practice as against theory, made on pragmatic practical grounds. "Socialist" Britain and "capitalist" United States have much more nearly identical economic systems than the doctrinaire economic philosophers of either would have one believe. The increasing opportunity for private enterprise will not occur if, as in Russia, there is a commitment to centralization of power for purposes of political control, brought about almost irreversibly by revolutionary means.

Therefore, although one must not fall into the error of employing our aid program to dictate another nation's economic philosophy, we can appropriately insist that we will aid only countries dedicated to advancing standards of living and encouraging widespread local initiative. With this condition, we need not be too concerned in the long run if some large-scale ventures are started under government auspices or if there is a preference for describing economic goals in socialist language.

Should Aid Stop Communism by Eliminating Hunger?

A final and serious misconception which exposes proposals for economic programs to attack is that revolt and protest are the result of hunger and poverty; that relieving hunger and reducing poverty will reduce revolutionary pressures; and that, therefore, if we can supply the wherewithal to feed people better, they are much less likely to support Communist or other extremist movements. Such reasoning is derived mainly from ignorance of the forces which bring about social and political change.

In the first place, the spirit of revolt does not breed easily among people who are chronically destitute. In the rigid feudal societies which still characterize some parts of the world the poor have for generations accepted a fatalistic view that it is in the nature of things that they should be poor; and people do not revolt when they believe change to be inherently impossible. At the grass roots of a feudal society one of the first effects of an economic development program is a dawning awareness that change can occur; and it is not poverty but this awareness combined with the energy-stimulating effects of better nutrition that is likely to release psychological and political pressures for change which may find expression in revolt. All this is well understood by the Communists, who concentrate their efforts not among those who are hopeless but among those in whom expectations have already been aroused. The Communist line is that these newly aroused expectations can never be satisfied except under revolutionary Communist leadership. This line is carefully tailored to whatever expectations and aspirations turn out to be most powerful in the particular people they are trying to influence. Moreover, once expectations have been aroused, a failure to do anything effective about them is grist to the Communist mill.

In the second place, even if the creation of wealth alone could satisfy a people's expectations, there is a limit to the rapidity with which economic development can increase national wealth and well-being. Under the most favorable conditions the maximum rate of growth of physical output likely to be achievable by countries in the early stages of development is 3 to 5 per cent per year. Where populations are increasing by 1½ to 2 per cent per year this means that the maximum rate of improvement of individual welfare is 2 or 3 per cent per year. But if growth is to become self-sustaining, some fraction of this increase must not be consumed: it must be set aside and plowed back into further investment. Therefore, the maximum rate of increase in consumption per person averaged over the population as a whole is not likely to exceed 1 or 2 per cent per year. It is true that even at a growth rate of only 1 per cent per year the standard of living will double in two generations and we should not ignore the importance one generation may attribute to prospects for improvement in the lot of its children, especially in peasant societies. And 1 per cent compounded over fifty years performs miracles, especially since, as the process goes on, the percentage will probably grow. But in the modern world of rapid communication political and social processes are greatly accelerated and will not give us fifty or even twenty years. The newly awakened peoples demand increasingly visible evidence of rapid progress.

Finally, most important, and wholly ignored by those who accept the crude materialist thesis that progress consists exclusively in "the extra food in the stomach," is the fact that an increase in consumption unaccompanied by many subtler changes in the society will not by itself guarantee orderly political development. This truth helps to explain the phenomenon which has been so puzzling to observers in a number of countries where Communist gains appear in some instances to have been greatest in areas where the government has been doing something about the economic problem rather than in those where nothing has been done.

Economic development efforts create potential unrest by dislodging convictions and habit patterns which have in the past insured stability. The education which accompanies economic change contributes to unrest. People who can't read can't be subverted by literature. Once they can read, the process of widening knowledge and changing ideas of what the world is like and what is possible in it proceeds with great rapidity. With a growing understanding of the great inequalities in the possession of wealth there is a growing awareness in backward societies that these inequalities are not the inevitable result of fate. In addition to this awareness there are other significant social and cultural effects of the very process of industrialization and urbanization. People brought up in the economic and psychological security of a traditional extended family system or a communal village structure are uprooted, moved to unfamiliar surroundings, plunged into a competitive world of individual effort with no paternalistic small group units to fall back on, and find their core values and beliefs subjected to daily challenge. They have a desperate need for new common goals and an experience of common effort and loyalties with some group which can give promise of re-establishing their confidence and their sense of private and social harmony. If these are not provided by the existing social and political structure, men and women will seek them in a dream of a wholly new structure provided, for example, by a locally adapted Communist line. It is certain that increase in material welfare alone will not satisfy spiritual and emotional needs.

It should be plain to us that if all that we have to offer to offset the disturbing effects of the breakdown of traditional cultures and the development of widely expanded expectations is the actual physical increment of new product created in two or three years by development, the picture is bleak indeed. Such a crude materialist conception of the way economic programs are supposed to work is not only wrong for the reasons given. It can be very dangerous. The conviction is already widespread in Asia that we value only physical consumption and have little or no understanding of things of the mind and spirit. If we promote economic programs based solely on a materialistic conception of progress, we shall not only be disappointed in their results but we shall also create additional hostility and contempt in the people we are trying to influence; and we may drive them to seek solutions more congenial to them than ours.

3 THE DEVELOPMENT OF MATURE DEMOCRACIES

IN THE FACE OF THE OBVIOUS possibility that the political and psychological effects of economic assistance programs can be contrary to our interests, would it not be better to leave the peoples of the underdeveloped areas of the world in a state of placid stagnation rather than arouse expectations that neither we nor they can possibly satisfy and thus expose their societies to the risk of social and political upheaval?

The question implies a choice that is not in fact open to us. The unprecedented spread of communication throughout the world in the last twenty years has already created new images of the future in the minds of the bulk of the world's population. The process of change is already inevitably and irreversibly under way, the expectations are already aroused, and the economic, political, and social revolution of the underdeveloped areas is already inexorably on the march. Even if the Communists were not everywhere promoting and encouraging this revolution in order to serve their own ends, its world-wide movement would be accelerated in the coming decades. The alternative of supporting semifeudal stability is a mirage.

Moreover, and even more to the point, there exists a powerful, positive case for an active promotion of economic development. The substance of this case can be found in the political, social, and psychological effects that a well-conceived economic development program can be made to have.

We have pointed out that one of the highest priority tasks for U.S. foreign policy is to use our influence to promote the evolution of societies that are stable in the sense that they are capable of rapid change without violence, effective in the sense that they can make progress in meeting the aspirations of all their citizens, and democratic in the sense that ultimate power is widely shared through the society. Such societies are not likely to constitute a military threat to us or to attach themselves to others who pose such a threat. Under modern circumstances some improvement in the standard of living, while not enough by itself, is certainly a necessary condition for the development of stable and peaceful societies and for the survival of democratic institutions. Even more important are the confidence generated by the sense of progress, the social mobility, the outlet for leadership energies, the national unity, the consolidation of new individual and group values, and discovery of new sources of satisfaction and achievement which a concentration of social and economic development can bring.

By actively promoting economic development in well-conceived programs of common action with the peoples of the new nations we can undertake to help them reach their goals. We can demonstrate more effectively than by any verbal propaganda the wide range of values we share with them. And in so doing we can use our margin of influence to move toward the realization of our own ultimate national interest—a world made up of free democratic societies.

The question, then, is not whether we should actively promote economic development programs but how such programs can serve to create such a world.

Before we can determine the role that economic programs can play, we must first be clear as to some of the principal requirements that must be met if the under-developed countries are to achieve political maturity.

A. *There must be posed for the leadership and the people of each country challenging and constructive internal tasks which will look to the future of their societies.* The peoples of the countries of Asia, the Middle East, and Africa have until recently been dominated by the will of foreign powers of different races from their own. It has been opposition to this external influence more than anything else which has given them a common purpose. Wherever they have achieved their independence from colonial control, this symbol of their common purpose has lost some if its energizing force. Many of them are trying to maintain and renew their sense of dedication and direction either by retrospectively fighting over again in their minds and in their political speeches the glorious revolutions they have already accomplished, or by identifying themselves with the revolutionary aspirations of countries still not independent. If they are to mature politically, these people must now turn their constructive energies on a broad scale to the real problems of their own internal future. Only when these problems of internal change have become the earnest concern of a large part of the population, and individuals throughout these societies see ways in which they can make useful contributions to the solution of these problems, will irresponsible extremist movements whose focus is on the battle symbols of the past lose their attraction and the institutions and forms of democracy become meaningful.

B. *The constructive tasks to which united national efforts are to be devoted must relate to the emerging aspirations of all classes and regions in the society.* The fight against international communism is neither sufficiently meaningful nor sufficiently related to the current hopes of most of the peoples of the underdeveloped areas to mobilize their political activity. First, it is a fight against and not a fight *for* something. Second, communism does not appear as a menace to the people in many of these areas because they have had no personal contact with what it can mean; and those who are aware of the struggle between the Communist bloc and the Free World regard it as something that matters to us but not to them. Third, since the Communists have very skillfully identified themselves with local causes, to attack communism in principle sometimes gives us the appearance of attacking the whole idea of trying to solve local problems. The best counter to Communist appeals is concrete demonstration that these same problems can be solved by other means than those the Communists propose. There must be in all parts of the society a rapid and increasing spread of the conviction that determined action within a democratic social order can make progress in attaining newly formulated goals.

C. *The new countries must find ways of developing young and vigorous leadership.* Many of their leaders are older men who have spent their lives organizing opposition or men selected by occupying powers either because they had a stake in the maintenance of the colonial system or because they could be trusted to administer without having too many ideas of their own. There are remarkable exceptions like Mr. Nehru who have been able to convey to their peoples an image of what their country might be like if they mobilize their human and material resources. But an expansion of the pool from which leadership can be drawn is everywhere a crying need. To develop the right kind of young leadership will require stressing problems which offer challenges and opportunities rather than threats, problems which appeal to creative rather than conservative instincts. There are reserves of leadership potential throughout the populations of the underdeveloped areas, but they must find a focus for their energies in problems they regard as real rather than symbolic.

D. *Related to the recruitment of new leadership is the*

need for greatly increased social, economic, and political opportunity. One reason for the widespread impression that leadership material is scarce in these countries is that the social class from which such leadership could traditionally be drawn has been pathetically small. One of the things the Communist movement does is to provide outlets for the awakening energies of young men previously denied opportunity by the rigid feudal class structure of their societies. Young leadership is in fact appearing. If it is denied opportunity to lead constructive programs, it will lead destructive ones. In particular, recruitment of non-Communist leadership has too frequently been confined to the cities, where a small fraction of the population is concentrated, while the human resources in the rural areas, where 70 to 90 per cent of the people in the under-developed countries live, have been largely untapped. Outsiders cannot force the recruitment of the potential young leadership in a country, but programs of rural development can uncover such potential.

E. *Related to this fact is the requirement, if these countries are to achieve mature political development, of finding ways to bridge the existing gulf between the urban classes, often Western educated, and the countryside.* In many instances the educated classes often know less—and, more important, care less—about their own countrymen in the rural districts than do we or other foreigners, a situation which has a doubly unfortunate influence. Where urban leaders do little about some of the country's most urgent problems, the mass of the people lack the conviction that their leaders are centrally concerned with their problems and aspirations. Those countries like India which are making the most progress toward maturity are those in which this gulf is being bridged—more through economic programs which yield a sense of common purpose derived from common effort than by any other means.

In this connection it is worth noting the special role played by the military in many of the underdeveloped countries. The army is frequently important to economic and political growth for three reasons. First, a military career is often the only way to positions of leadership and responsibility open to members of the less privileged classes and especially to men with rural backgrounds. The military is thus often a good source from which to draw new leaders for nonmilitary programs. Second, the army is often the only career in which a man has an opportunity to acquire both technical and administrative skills. Many of these skills are easily transferable to such civilian tasks as the building of roads and communication systems or the organization of a local community for improved sanitation. Third, military service provides vocational training which gives the peasants the skills needed in industry. Countries which have adopted military conscription might well pay more attention to the constructive potentialities of such a system.

When we speak of recruiting new leadership, we do not mean solely or even primarily leadership at the national political level. Local, regional, and functional leadership are at least as crucial to orderly development. Indeed, in discussing the development of democratic societies there is a tendency to think too largely in terms of the mechanical process by which national leadership is chosen. Power and decision-making cannot be decentralized, whatever the electoral process, unless at lower levels there are competent and dedicated people available to whom decisions can be delegated. A country which is formally a dictatorship but whose government encourages local and group initiatives and is responsive to them may be more democratic than one which goes through the motions of national elections but has no political vigor at the grass roots. Since the problems of maintaining national cohesion in the face of rapid social and economic change are so unsettling, the newly independent countries may have to pass through a variety of transitional political forms in their search for a democratic framework appropriate to their own situation. The crucial test is whether local leadership and local participation in decisions of local interest are being nurtured.

F. *Perhaps the most critical requirement for the growth of political maturity is that the people of the new nations develop confidence, both as a nation and as individuals in small communities, that they can make progress with their problems through their own efforts.* The principal reason for believing that some growth in economic output, even at a slow rate, is critically important to political stability is that such growth has become for people in all the new nations an increasingly important symbol of their capabilities, their national worth, and their national dignity. If this growth is widespread through the country and based upon a good measure of local community initiative, it can become a vital symbol of individual and community as well as national achievement. The Communists are saying through the countryside, "Your leaders are bankrupt. You can do nothing under the present system to work toward the satisfaction of your hopes. Join us and we will give you a meaningful mission." There must be a creative alternative to this appeal if democratic evolution is to succeed.

It should be emphasized also that a sense of confidence is the chief prerequisite for the development of satisfactory external relations with the rest of the world. At the moment many of these new nations are fearful that other nations have objectives and values different from their own which threaten their national integrity and security. Once they see that they are wholly capable of standing on their own feet, they can afford to be less quixotic and nervous in their foreign policies. A confident nation, making progress at home, is likely to conduct its foreign policy with poise and good sense.

4 WHAT AN ECONOMIC PROGRAM CAN DO

IT SHOULD BE APPARENT THAT whether economic programs have desirable political and psychological effects in terms of the principal requirements for the growth of political maturity will depend on how they are carried through. We have had experience with aid programs which justify all the scornful strictures of their opponents, and which have been not merely neutral in their effect and hence wasteful but positively harmful to our interests. We have learned that benefits do not follow any more automatically from the voting of sums of money by the Congress in this field of policy than in any other. But past mistakes do not alter the basic fact that economic programs are one of our few potentially effective levers of influence upon political developments in the underdeveloped areas.

Why is this so? The answer lies in the social and political connotations of the economic growth process.

A Constructive Outlet for Nationalism

The possibility of economic growth presents a real challenge to the constructive energies of the people of the newly independent nations. Some, like India, have already demonstrated that this challenge can have much greater appeal as a rallying point for national effort than the preservation of their societies from what we believe to be an external threat. Indeed, in India the problems of internal development have already started to replace colonialism, race discrimination, and relations with foreign countries as the burning issues of national and local politics. The present government has tied its fortunes to the success of its five-year plans and has generated a remarkable degree of interest in them, even in the remote villages. Performance under the five-year plans has become important not merely as an index of the effectiveness of the present government but as a major symbol of Indian national aspirations, independence, and dignity. A realization of forward movement in this effort, even if the visible economic results are not spectacular, has become a prime factor in the national consciousness. There is, moreover, a widespread awareness among Indians of India's competition in growth with Communist China. It is not accidental that India's internal political situation, though not free of disturbing elements, is better than that of most other Asian countries. India's effective absorption in a constructive economic effort is not the whole explanation of her relative political success, but it is such an important element that a reversal of the present favorable trend could lead to a rapid deterioration in the political scene. It is plain that if we support efforts like the Indian one and encourage the development of such efforts in other countries we can help strengthen the authentic human striving for the values of democracy which, sometimes beneath the surface, characterizes virtually all the new nations.

A Social Solvent

More specifically, development assistance can be made conditional upon the submission of convincing evidence that a country's leaders have thought through the needs of all sectors of their population. The urban-educated elite tends to think first in terms of factories and other urban-centered activities. Requirements of economic balance can literally force such leaders to go out into the countryside where the bulk of their people live and learn what rural conditions and prospects really are. Indian intellectuals are learning, slowly but surely, to work with peasants, to use their hands, to interest themselves in the issues peculiar to their own nation rather than in the intellectual fashions of the Western world. As a result, although there are still villages in India where people have never heard of Nehru, much less of community development, the number of these is shrinking with amazing rapidity. A more energetic focus on development, accompanied by an insistence on balanced programs, could have similar effects in countries where the gap between city and country is still almost unbridged and where the Communists and other instigators of violence therefore have a clear field in the rural areas.

The Development of Leadership

One of the significant aspects of programs of agricultural and village development programs is that they probably provide the best opportunities for uncovering and encouraging new sources of young leadership. The village worker-training programs which several countries in Asia are undertaking are recruiting from sectors of the population outside of the castes and classes to which opportunity has traditionally been limited. Even in the cities, industrial development is beginning to be accompanied in a few places by a labor movement that is shifting its focus from political agitation to increasingly responsible concern with the economic welfare of the working classes within the framework of existing institutions. This process has a long way to go, but it is moving in the right direction. The failure of efforts at economic growth could rapidly reverse this trend and drive labor and peasant organizations back to a concentration on political protest instead of constructive effort. More vigorous promotion of growth with opportunities for these groups to realize some success in their efforts to improve their welfare could greatly accelerate the emergence of responsibility in such organizations.

Confidence in the Democratic Process

Psychologically, as was pointed out above, confidence that individual men and women have it in their power to improve their own lot is one of the most essential requirements for political responsibility. Economic evidences of success are among the most persuasive ones. People become confident as they see new factories, better farming methods, improved public health and education, and better transport come into being in response to their own efforts. The wider the participation in such acts of construction, the more likely is the political effect to be salutary.

Finally, many kinds of economic programs provide opportunities to demonstrate political democracy in action which are much more convincing than either abstract discussion or the operation of electoral machinery divorced from real problems. If people are to regard voting as more than a symbolic gesture, they must have something to vote about which directly concerns them, and they must have candidates whose appeal is related to recognizable issues rather than to oratorical gift and a wide circle of acquaintances. Economic issues are, of course, not the only ones with real vitality, but in countries where a majority of the people live close to the margin of brute poverty, most cultural, educational, and social issues are directly related to economic problems. Village education requires schools, equipment, and the support of teachers; public health requires medical services, better nutrition, and better housing; social justice frequently depends on land redistribution and community services; a wider communication of ideas demands roads, radio, films and, above all, literacy and the written word that then comes to life.

International Solidarity

International co-operation on economic issues offers opportunities to demonstrate not only the common goals shared by the peoples of one country with those of another but also helpful ways in which those goals are being pursued abroad. Such demonstrations correct false images of foreign societies. One of the most politically effective programs we have carried out to date has been the sponsoring of visits to American industry by European productivity teams. The ostensible purpose of these visits was to give the visitors new ideas about technical and organizational ways to increase productivity. Their most dramatic consequence, widely attested to, was to spread an understanding of what labor-management relations are really like in America. Visitor after visitor from both European management and labor expressed amazement at the degree of democracy and mutual human respect they found in American labor-management relations.

Ideology, values, and principles of political organization can be much more quickly grasped and promoted through programs of common action than through debate or "education." In advising and consulting on labor-management relations, on the organization of co-operatives, on agricultural extension, on educational methods, on land reform, on local government, on training and recruitment of specialists, managers, foremen, civil servants and administrators, the United States has endless opportunities to illustrate the practical application of American values, unobscured by unfamiliar ideological terminology.

It is perhaps necessary to repeat that economic problems are not the only focus for constructive effort. But almost all the challenging things people can be stirred to want to do for themselves and their societies require some additional resources. Without economic growth neither the human energies nor the physical resources required to satisfy the aspirations of their peoples will be available to the poorer countries of the world. Not only is economic growth a prerequisite for political, cultural, and social improvement, it can also be an engine of such improvement.

The American Objective Restated

We Americans have a unique opportunity. We alone in all the world have the resources to make steady and substantial economic growth an active possibility for the underdeveloped nations of the Free World. But our basic objectives are political rather than economic. They are political in the sense that our most pressing interest is to help the societies of the world develop in ways that will not menace our security—either as a result of their own internal dynamics or because they are weak enough to be used as tools by others. But our ability to influence political development by direct argument or intervention is very slight. Indeed, direct political intervention is almost certain to set up resentments and resistances which will produce the exact reverse of the result we seek. Economic programs which are neutral with respect to the political issues which rouse men's passions nonetheless can be effective instruments of political influence—not because they will recruit allies, but in a much more fundamental sense because they can develop political responsibility. They are thus a way—we would argue the best and perhaps the only way—around the impasse which confronts us when we try to use our political influence directly.

An important illustration of this principle is to be found in our policies toward colonialism. We should be more vigorously on the side of freedom and independence for subject peoples. But, leaving aside the difficulties of direct political intervention in the affairs of our European allies, it is not at all clear that we contribute to the peace and stability of the world by encouraging colonial peoples to rally their energies around the goal of violent revolution. There is some merit in the argument of the colonial powers that to turn loose their colonies before they have acquired the capacity to deal with their own affairs is to do the colonies as well as the world at large a disservice.

On the other hand, it would be hard for the colonial powers to deny that a vigorous and world-wide program of assistance to economic development must logically include the colonial areas. We can and should apply the same conditions to these as to other recipients of assistance, notably, that responsibility for economic programs must be accepted by the people of the area themselves at both local and national levels. We can insist, through economic programs, on seeking out and developing local leadership. We can make a persuasive case to the occupying powers that such programs will provide an outlet for the energies of local communities which will reduce their preoccupation with subversion and violence against Europeans. We can with equal justice insist that our aim in supporting these programs is to speed the time at which the colonial peoples can secure that independence to which we as well as they are dedicated. We can show the peoples of the colonies that we are effectively hastening the day of independence for them by forcing, as a technically necessary condition for economic growth, the delegation to them of an increasingly important share of the decisions that affect their daily lives and welfare. Thus the formal status of political independence will become emotionally less urgent and more attainable. To describe all the ways in which this can be done would take more space than we can devote to it here. But we are convinced that a skillful program of economic and technical assistance could both accelerate independence and take much of the dynamite out of the symbols of colonialism if it is pursued with vigor and imagination well before the dynamite has begun to explode.

The impact of such a program on the economies of the developed countries of the Free World will be discussed later. Equally important, however, are the possible political and psychological effects on the other developed nations of a program of development in which they participate as partners. Our common efforts with them to date, with the notable exception of the Marshall Plan, have been largely military and have had the vital but negative objective of confining the expansion of Communist military power. Given the role of atomic weapons in modern warfare and the preponderant strength of the United States in these weapons and the means of their delivery, our European allies feel themselves in an awkward dependent position, worried observers of the American-Soviet arms race on which their security depends but to the outcome of which they can only marginally contribute. It is important for our relations with them that we demonstrate that we regard the Free World as an enterprise in construction within which they can and must share in major tasks. A joint effort to help build successful democratic societies in the underdeveloped areas could strengthen the American-European alliance, by adding to the binding force of fear the cement of hope.

5 THE STAGES OF GROWTH

The Pattern of Experience

IT IS ARGUED IN THE PRECEDING chapters that it is in the American interest to do what we can to support the efforts of the underdeveloped countries to develop their economies. Any detailed program to serve this purpose must be based upon an understanding of the economic problems these countries face and of the possibilities and limitations of the influence outsiders can exert in helping them to solve these problems. No two of these countries are alike, and the problems of growth will be shaped in each by its resources, its culture, its history, and its political institutions. Nonetheless, there is emerging from the intensive work of social scientists on the development problem a recognition that there are common elements in the patterns of development of different countries which have implications for development policy everywhere. Since our proposals grow out of our conception of some of these common elements, it is important to try to summarize them.

Once societies are stirred from the lethargy of traditional economic stagnation, their transition to mature self-sustained growth can be divided into three stages.

Establishing the Preconditions

First, there is a period during which the preconditions for economic progress are established. The idea spreads that economic progress is possible. Education, for some at least, broadens and changes to suit the needs of modern economic activity. Enterprising men emerge willing to mobilize savings and to take risks in pursuit of profit. Institutions for mobilizing capital appear. Basic capital is expanded, notably in transport, communications, and products such as raw materials, which can be sold in export trade. The orbit of commerce, internal and external, widens. And, here and there, manufacturing enterprises are started. But all this activity proceeds on a limited basis within an economy and a society still characterized by traditional low-productivity techniques and by the old values and institutions which developed in conjunction with them.

During this period, which generally lasts some time, two obstacles stand in the way of more rapid growth. The first is that these countries are desperately poor and the margin above bare subsistence is small. They must learn to channel this small margin into productive investment before they can get off dead center. This often requires important political and social change and takes time. In the meanwhile, virtually the entire output of their economies is required merely to keep their populations alive on a miserable pittance. Indeed, when bad harvests or other misfortunes occur, even this is not possible and widespread starvation is likely. In good years it may be possible to set aside a small part of output for future use, but any impetus this gives to growth is likely to be wiped out by a few bad years. Thus the precondition stage is commonly marked by a series of false starts in which some early signs of growth appear, only to wither later, as the economy returns to stagnation.

The second obstacle is that, even if capital is available from outside, the capacity to absorb it in many sectors of the economy is very low. It does little good to supply money to build plants if there are no skilled workers to operate them, no competent administrators to manage them, inadequate transport to bring in their raw materials and carry away their product, no repair facilities to maintain them, inadequate power to run them, and insufficient purchasing power to buy what they produce. To some extent skills and knowledge can be provided from outside along with financial resources, but the take-off into continuing growth cannot occur until certain minimum preconditions of education, skills and attitudes, and basic transportation, communication, and power facilities have been established. Included among the preconditions is the establishment of reasonably effective government and civil order. Roughly this precondition stage lasted in Great Britain until about 1783, in Japan until 1880, in Russia until around 1890, and has lasted in Indonesia up to the present.

Did the United States have to go through this process of establishing the preconditions for growth? Yes. The United States belongs among a small group of countries which were well endowed with rich agricultural land and relatively small populations, like New Zealand, Australia, and Canada. It took the United States from about 1790 to 1840 to establish the preconditions; but unlike the underdeveloped nations of the modern world Americans ate well and enjoyed a relatively high standard of living in the period before the take-off.

The Take-off

Following this precondition stage there comes a second stage during which the country makes the complex transition to a position where sustained economic growth becomes possible. Under the impact of a particular stimulus, sometimes technological, sometimes political, the economy lurches forward. The forces for economic progress, which up to now have yielded limited bursts of activity, expand and become decisive factors. The rate of savings—that part of its product a country plows back into its own future growth—rises from, say, 5 per cent of the national income to 10 per cent or more. Even more important is the mechanism by which this occurs. The economy organizes itself so that a high proportion (25 to 50 per cent) of any increase in output is plowed back into further investment. New key industries expand rapidly, yielding profits of which a large share is reinvested in new capacity. New techniques spread in both agriculture and industry as increasing numbers of people are prepared to accept them and the deep changes they bring to ways of life. A new class of businessmen (usually private, sometimes public servants) emerges and acquires control over the key decisions determining the use of savings. New possibilities for export and new import requirements develop. The economy exploits unused backlogs in technique and natural resources.

This is the stage when the need for foreign capital is at its peak. Often, particularly toward the end of this stage, the burgeoning enterprise attracts substantial private capital from other countries. In a decade or two the basic structure of the economy and the social and political structure of the society are transformed in such a way that a steady rate of growth can be sustained with a diminishing inflow of capital. Roughly, this was the process through which Britain had passed by 1815, the United States by 1860, Japan by 1900, Russia by 1913, and through which India seeks to pass in the next decade or so.

Self-Sustained Growth

Third comes the long period of regular if fluctuating progress. Some 10 to 20 per cent of the national income is steadily plowed back into expanding productive capacity. The structure of the economy changes continuously—sometimes painfully—as technique improves. The economy of the country becomes more intimately related to the international economy and may, from time to time, face difficult balance of payments problems. The society makes its terms with the requirements of modern and efficient production. As rapid growth provides the margin of resources from which additional investment can be made, the need for capital from abroad slackens; ultimately it ceases entirely, and domestic savings become so abundant that they begin to seek profitable employment abroad in economies even more recently launched on the growth sequence.

Underdevelopment Clarified

In the contemporary world the so-called underdeveloped countries stand at different points in relation to the three stages of economic growth. Most of the countries of central Africa and the Middle East and a few in Latin America like Bolivia and Ecuador have barely begun to develop the preconditions for the transition to growth. Others, like Indonesia, and perhaps Peru and Iran, are approaching a point where a sustained effort to make the transition may become feasible within, say, a decade. India, Burma, and the Philippines are beginning the transition, and Mexico may be emerging from it. A few like Argentina and, possibly, Turkey have, on the whole, passed through this transition with success and now confront the problems of regular growth itself, which often involves (as in these two cases) painful structural adjustments.

To determine the stage in which a country finds itself, two indices are useful. If a country has maintained an average rate of growth of per capita income of at least 1 or 2 per cent per year over at least a five-year period, and if this cannot be explained by adventitious events such as a series of exceptionally favorable crops, or abnormally high prices for its exports, this is good evidence that it is passing from the precondition stage into the stage of transition. A further test, though this may be statistically hard to determine, is what proportion of its annual product it is able to set aside for investment purposes. In the precondition stage this is unlikely to be more than 5 or 6 per cent. During the transition it climbs until in the third stage it reaches 15 per cent or better. Of course, these statistical tests are only indicators which must be interpreted in the light of a fuller examination of the characteristics of the economy and the whole society of which it is a part by someone intimately familiar with the way that society operates; but the statistical tests provide useful rules of thumb.

The assistance which countries need from outside if they are to develop is of two kinds. In the first place they need capital, both to establish the preconditions of growth and to make sure during the second stage that growth is maintained until they reach a point where they can be reasonably sure of maintaining it out of their own increasing output. Underdeveloped countries may require two sorts of capital. They will need from outside some of the equipment and supplies required to construct particular development projects. They will also frequently need a certain volume of food and consumer goods to permit them to divert their own labor and other resources from output for consumption to development. But in addition to capital they will also need a great deal of technical assistance, a transfer of knowledge and skills from other parts of the world, to permit them to make effective use both of their own meagre supplies of capital and of whatever capital is made available from abroad.

Policy Implications

The capital and technical assistance needs of a Free World growth program will reflect these different stages of growth and, therefore, the different requirements of the various countries involved. At an early stage, basic education may be the prime requirement in many countries, and in others such overhead capital as ports and railways. In many, technical assistance of various kinds may be more urgently needed than capital. In a few, industrial capital equipment itself may be the urgent prerequisite for continued progress. Programs for most countries should have all these elements within them, in different degrees. Each country must work out its program individually. There are no general rules of thumb such as the balance of payments deficits which so powerfully affected Marshall Plan allocations.

The different stages of growth have several important implications for foreign economic policy. The first is that substantial outside capital can be productively used by an

economy in the first or precondition stage only in a few
fields like transport, irrigation, mining, and power. Some
capital can be absorbed in agriculture and industry, but
the amounts will be quite small. In the transition stage,
opportunities for productive investment spread to more
and more kinds of activity, but there continue to be sharp,
if continually rising, limits on how much can be absorbed.
These limits on the amounts that can be productively used,
sometimes termed the technical absorptive capacity, are
set by such factors as the technical and a managerial
capacity available, the size, stability, and motivations of
the nonagricultural labor force, the level of skills and education, the development of markets, the state of basic
facilities for transport, communications, power, and community services. In the third stage technical absorptive
capacity ceases to be a limiting factor on the volume of
investment, which is then limited rather by how much of
its output the economy is willing to set aside for investment
and how much it can borrow in normal international capital markets.

Certain limited types of investment, such as in the production of raw materials for export, depend for their productivity not on the state of the domestic economy but on
the level of demand in world markets. Oil wells can be
drilled, rubber plantations established, tin mines opened
by foreign capital with foreign technicians, largely irrespec-
tive of technical absorptive capacity. But for precisely this
reason the impact of investment of this kind on the domestic economy of the country or on its capacity for general

development is likely to be small. With these types of investment, which existing private capital can be relied upon to undertake and which contribute little to broad development, we are not here particularly concerned. But outlets for investment to serve domestic markets or to supply domestic industry will be very limited in the early stages. This does not mean that large projects will never be required by countries in the first stage. Certain types of investment in transport, irrigation, power, and the like may have to be undertaken before there is any evidence that the economy as a whole has begun to expand. As a rule, management talent for such projects will have to be supplied. Thus, it would not take a very large program to supply all the capital requirements of the presently under-developed areas under suitable criteria of absorptive capacity.

Second, the principal risks attending investment in under-developed areas are those associated with the question of whether or not the economy will in fact grow continuously in the future. These risks are highest in the precondition stage. It is difficult to predict with precision when the take-off will occur or how much capital will have to be supplied before it will take place. These risks are so great that no more than a fraction of the needed resources can probably be supplied on a loan basis to countries in the first stage. The bulk of it will have to be grants and technical assistance. But again, because absorptive capacity in this stage is low, and only a limited number of projects justify the risk, the magnitude of grants need not be very great.

When the country reaches the take-off stage, its absorptive capacity goes up and the risks of repayment go down. The whole program may, of course, fail; but a better evaluation of that chance is possible. In this stage an investment program can shift from a grant to a loan basis, but to achieve the objective of the program, the loans must carry longer maturities and lower rates of interest than would obtain for comparable investments in developed economies. Since they involve estimates of the future performance of the whole economy, many of the risks are of a sort that private investors cannot be expected to bear. In this second stage, therefore, when a substantial amount of external capital must be supplied if the country is to get over the hump, this capital must be supplied in part at least by other than private investors. This is so both because the risks are higher and because the terms must be more favorable to the borrower than they would have to be for alternative investments in the developed countries. It is worth exploring whether devices could not be worked out for supplying capital from public sources on an equity basis to countries in this stage, repayment and interest to be contingent on a minimum rate of growth of the national product.

Finally, when the country has demonstrated its capacity for growth, two factors reduce the requirement for extraordinary channels for the provision of outside capital. First, the country is now generating out of its own rising output the resources to plow back into its own capital formation; and, second, investment opportunities are emerging which compare favorably in profit prospects with those in other developed countries. Thus the normal channels of international capital supply can be relied on to take over the burden of any net capital inflow still required.

In summary, then, in the precondition stage the demands for capital are low because of severely limited capacity to absorb it. In the second stage they are a good deal higher, though compared with levels of investment in developed countries they will still be small. But this second stage is in any case of limited duration, say ten or fifteen years, and the supplying countries can look forward to a time when extraordinary measures to insure capital from outside can be discontinued.

In the light of this analysis it is essential to note that the proposals set forth in this paper do not open the United States up to an endless, open-ended, world-wide claim on its resources. The American purpose would be to assist countries in establishing the preconditions for growth (mainly through technical assistance) and to assist them with capital, notably in the decisive period of transition. The objective is not to redistribute income as between the industrialized and underdeveloped nations: the objective is to help the underdeveloped nations into the stage of self-sustained growth. When a country has passed the transition, it should be in a position to operate on its own with help only from normal international capital market institutions.

6 THE PROPOSAL

Partnership for Economic Growth

THE CENTRAL PROPOSAL OF THIS
book is that the United States should, for reasons stated
in Chapter 1, take the leadership in a new international
partnership program for world economic growth.

The strictly economic purposes of the program would
be: first, to make available sufficient capital to permit the
low-income countries to launch an ultimately self-sustaining process of economic development; second, to stimulate
and assist the underdeveloped countries to overcome
obstacles to their own development other than lack of
capital; and third, to create a climate of international
economic activity in which the economies of the industrialized countries of Europe and Japan, as well as the United
States, could continue to grow.

Fundamental to the proposal is the thesis, explained in the preceding chapter, that there is a particularly critical period in the economic development of every country which determines whether that country will emerge into a long-run process of growth with expanding levels of per capita welfare or sink back into economic stagnation at the margin of subsistence. If it does the former, there is hope that the political results described in Chapter 3 will follow. If it does the latter, the probabilities of political chaos and instability—giving way to some form of totalitarian government—are very high. External capital is required to prepare countries for the transition to self-sustained long-run economic growth. In the transition itself external capital will often make the critical difference between an upward spiral of economic, social, and political development and a downward spiral of stagnation and decay.

More specifically, what we propose is that the United States, in participation with the other developed nations, should give assurance to every underdeveloped Free World country that it can secure as much capital as it can use productively in accordance with strict criteria of productivity. Countries would be divided into three categories: (1) those in the precondition stage, which would be offered an expanded volume of technical assistance and such capital as they could demonstrate they were ready for, much of it on a grant basis; (2) those in the transition stage, which would be offered continued technical assistance and as much capital as they could well absorb and wished to borrow at favorable rates of interest and with long maturities, provided the proposed programs and projects met agreed criteria of productivity; and (3) those which have achieved self-sustaining growth, whose access to foreign capital would be determined by their credit worthiness as judged by existing international sources, private and public.

We believe, as explained in Chapter 10, that the amounts which would be taken up under such an offer over the next ten years or so would not at the most be more than two or three billion dollars a year higher than current levels of international capital movement. Only a portion of that amount would need to be in the form of funds provided by the U.S. government. A major fraction of that portion could be in the form of loans rather than grants, and a part of it (15 to 25 per cent) could be supplied in the form of U.S. agricultural surpluses.

A Banking Concept

Aside from its scale several elements of this proposal distinguish it from past practice. One of these key characteristics is that every request for assistance which met criteria of productivity, to be described later, would be granted. In the early stages some countries—India, for example—which are at a stage of development where they can readily absorb additional capital would get the lion's share. As other countries were able to demonstrate that they were establishing new institutions to carry on economic activity, developing a labor force with the necessary skills, training administrators and managers capable of operating new ventures, and drawing up detailed investment programs to insure balanced and consistent growth, they would become eligible for higher levels of assistance. Meanwhile, as incomes rose in the faster moving countries, they would begin to find themselves in a position to supply a larger and larger part of their capital requirements out of their own savings.

The essential idea of this program is that the allocation of funds would be based on a banking concept rather than a subsidy concept. A banker does not list all his potential customers and then try to decide how to allocate his loanable funds in such a way as to be fair to each. He sets certain criteria for the soundness of loans and then welcomes all customers who can satisfy him that they meet the criteria. As explained later, the criteria in this program would be somewhat broader than those normally applied by a bank. They would relate not merely to the soundness of each particular project taken by itself but also to the prospects for the entire economy in which the project was to be located. But the distribution of funds among countries would be determined by absorptive capacity rather than by considerations of equity or politics.

Built-in Incentives

A second key characteristic of the proposal is that it is designed to provide maximum incentives to the governments of the underdeveloped countries to take the steps necessary to promote development and thus make their countries eligible for assistance. It is a fundamental assumption of this program that the development of capacity to use capital effectively to promote growth is a job mainly for the underdeveloped countries themselves. A properly designed world program of technical assistance can help greatly in supplying the know-how and in carrying out the needed national programs of training and education. Present technical assistance programs should be suitably expanded to this end; and the task of a new program should be not merely to make more capital available but also to advise and assist countries in preparing themselves to use capital productively. But the bulk of the task must be done by the people of the developing country itself. They must develop the necessary institutions, generate the required energy and initiative, acquire the requisite wisdom and courage in planning and controlling resource use, learn the necessary skills and techniques.

The partnership program here proposed would remove the one bottleneck over which the underdeveloped countries cannot have much control—lack of capital. If the program were adopted, with the announced intention of maintaining it for some time, each Free World country would know that whenever and wherever it was able to demonstrate that it could use resources productively in the context of a sensible national program, the resources would be made available without any sort of military or political strings. The impact of this knowledge, consistently at work over a period of years, would be a powerful force pushing countries to take the steps needed for their own growth.

The program we propose would place the burden of responsibility for economic growth squarely on the underdeveloped countries themselves. At present, political leaders in these countries can excuse their own failures to themselves and to their constituents on the ground that their national resources are simply not equal to the task, and that the richer countries refuse to help on terms they can accept. But if over a period of years the internal prerequisites for effective and productive use of capital are continually reiterated by a respected and impartial international body, and if the knowledge spreads that loans or grants necessary to progress will be forthcoming wherever and whenever adequate steps are being taken to achieve these prerequisites, the pressure on government for effective performance will become irresistible.

The Development of Absorptive Capacity

It is basic to our analysis that if the program we propose were accepted, economic growth in many areas would depend more on the development of absorptive capacity than on the availability of capital funds. A third key element is, then, that the program provide for the expansion of absorptive capacity. To develop absorptive capacity in its widest sense is the basic function of technical assistance. We recommend, therefore, that existing technical assistance programs be reviewed in the light of the experience of the past decade and if necessary expanded, and that they be purposefully reshaped to mesh with the proposed program of loans and grants. In general, where the bulk of a country's loan or grant applications fail to meet the proposed criteria, a *prima facie* case for expanded technical assistance would exist.

There are several kinds of technical assistance which may deserve more priority and resources than they have hitherto been given.

A. We have emphasized the great importance for the underdeveloped countries of working out consistent and detailed national development programs. In the early stages and for many countries the lack of such well-considered programs will be a principal limitation on their ability to absorb loans and grants. In recent years the pool of talent and experience in programming techniques has been growing rapidly. It should be possible to supply countries just starting the programming process with technical assistance which could greatly accelerate their progress.

B. One of the most serious bottlenecks inhibiting the development of absorptive capacity in the underdeveloped countries is a shortage of managerial and administrative skills. Two kinds of assistance would be useful here. The first would help establish educational and training programs designed to increase the supply of indigenous managerial and administrative talent. The second would help meet the interim deficiency in such talent by providing foreign managerial skill under arrangements which would not compromise domestic control. The recent experience of foreign management contracts has generally been encouraging, and the possibility of a radical expansion of this device is worth exploration.

C. Existing technical assistance programs under both U.S. and U.N. auspices are already making available much engineering advice. If the plan we propose is adopted, the needs for such assistance will expand greatly. Some thought should be given to the organization of an international pool of engineering experts with experience in the problems of adapting engineering design to the conditions present in underdeveloped areas. Such a pool, in addition to providing consultants on request, might conduct research into problems of engineering design common to a number of countries.

D. More fundamentally, a purposeful effort should be made to apply new scientific knowledge to the economic problems of the underdeveloped areas. One of the resources in which the United States is richest, our scientific skill and imagination, has been of necessity rather heavily focused in recent years on the development of weapons. Many of our top scientists would eagerly welcome an opportunity to turn their energies to constructive problems relating to human welfare. The same kind of concentration of first-class minds on a specific problem that has produced one breakthrough after another in military technology should be capable of opening some of the technological bottlenecks to growth in the underdeveloped areas.

The arrangements being set up for the development of atomic energy for peacetime uses could be made the focal point for a more general co-operative scientific program. Peacetime use of atomic energy is only one of many exciting new technical developments which should be pursued. Imaginative effort on an adequate scale might well produce important developments on such problems as making fresh water from sea water at low cost, rainfall control, the capture and use of solar energy, the development of algae as food sources, and chemical means of population control. Regional laboratories or institutes could be established to work on these problems, and scientists and engineers from the entire Free World could be brought to them.

The Well-Understood Objective

A fourth such key element is that the recipient countries must be convinced that the program does not have narrowly political or military objectives. Its basic political objective— the development of stable, effective societies moving in a democratic direction—is one with which no non-Communist country will quarrel. But if it is believed that the program is designed to force neutrals into our camp, to secure acceptance of particular American foreign policies, or to draw other countries into conflicts which they believe, however rightly or wrongly, do not concern them, none of the more fundamental results we seek will be secured. The underdeveloped countries, many of them recently fresh from successful efforts to throw off political domination by colonial powers, are highly sensitive about their political independence. If they believe their independence will be compromised by accepting assistance from us, either in grant or in loan form, they will reject that assistance, as some of them have already done in the past, however desperately they need it for their own growth. Many of them believe that if assistance is channeled through an international body, they will be better protected from political interference. How far we can or should accept this view is discussed in Chapter 11. But the fact remains that unless we are crystal clear in our own minds that our purposes in undertaking this particular program are neither to strengthen the military forces of our allies nor to buy adherence to our foreign policies, no international institution can protect the program from our misconceptions. If we do achieve consensus and clarity on this point in the United States, international safeguards become much less crucial.

The Positive Criteria

It is, of course, as important to have agreed positive criteria of eligibility as it is not to apply wrong criteria. Our purpose is not a giveaway program without strings of any kind. We have a very specific purpose in adopting such a program: to promote the economic growth of the underdeveloped countries; and we should be very sure that any money we make available, in either grant or loan form, will serve that purpose. We believe, as explained further in Chapter 7, that a set of criteria can be established which will have the agreement and respect of both the recipient countries and the participating suppliers of capital. These should include the general conditions that development be undertaken for the benefit of the entire population of the recipient country and that the goals of its development program be related to the aspirations of all of its people. Beyond this, they should include quite severe technical conditions governing the economic effectiveness of assistance in promoting development. Programming discussions must result in agreement that the recipient country has worked out: (1) a consistent national development program, (2) practical ways of implementing it with available skills and facilities, and (3) effective ways of mobilizing the country's own national resources, including a high rate of saving for development. The application of these criteria will require great judgment, skill, and understanding. No formal set of rules can substitute for wise administration. Nonetheless, the subject of criteria is such a sensitive one that we believe an effort to develop an explicit code of ground rules for an assistance program is worth while. The United States agencies responsible for this program should set up such a code to govern their own behavior and should discuss this code both with participating suppliers of capital and with recipients.

International Sponsorship

Related to this is another key element of the program; namely, that its sponsorship should be international rather than national. This does not mean that all administration of the program must be turned over to the United Nations or some other international organization. There are many countries now contributing to development assistance through many agencies, both national and international. Each has its own approach and function and no purpose would be served by consolidating them all. It is quite possible, however, to retain a large number of separate channels of financing and at the same time bring them all within the framework of an internationally agreed program. We have already suggested the desirability of establishing an international code of criteria which would set the basic philosophy and ground rules to which both supplying and recipient countries would adhere. This could be supported by an international secretariat, perhaps broken down into regional commissions, to maintain information, review programs, co-ordinate various elements in the international flow of capital, and act as a broker between countries needing assistance and those who might supply it.

A significant degree of internationalization could strengthen the program in another, nontechnical respect. It could contribute to the sense that the countries of the world were engaged in a great common constructive effort. This is as important to the morale of the industrialized countries as to that of the underdeveloped nations.

A World-Wide Program

We believe the incentive effects of the plan will be much more pronounced if it is applied on a world scale rather than if it is limited to one or two regions of the world like Southeast Asia and the Middle East. It should be clear from what has gone before that we do not think it should be labeled as an anti-Communist or anti-Soviet program. In the long run we are as interested in stability and growth in Africa and Latin America as in Asia. Since much of Africa consists of colonies, it is impossible to launch an African program without the support of the colonial powers. That support is most likely to be forthcoming for an effort embracing the whole Free World. Within a global program, Africa clearly deserves a place, and many of the conditions which should be set down for programs elsewhere can and should be applied there. This does not mean, of course, that all planning and administration must be on a global basis. Regional units are both more meaningful and more efficient. But once again, the philosophy and ground rules of the program would gain great support from being placed in a global context.

Continuity

Lastly, the program will have very little incentive effect if it is not assured of continuity over a number of years. The steps that must be taken to prepare a country for effective use of additional investment resources are complex, time consuming, and difficult. If an offer of assistance is to stimulate action in compliance with its conditions, it must be a standing offer effective over an extended period. Even where the general environmental conditions are already favorable, project planning and the adjustment of development programs may require two or three years. Where more fundamental deficiencies in education, statis-

tical information, labor and entrepreneurial skills, transport
and communications, and public administration exist, the
lead time may be a decade or more. Even quite a large
program will lose most of its effectiveness if it teeters along
on the verge of Congressional disapproval with no more
than a one-year lease on life. The limited magnitude and
great uncertainty of our programs for the underdeveloped
areas to date go far to explain the lack of response to such
offers as the President's special fund for Asian regional
development.

Avoiding Autarchy

Finally, there are two other key aspects of this proposal.
First, though the underdeveloped countries will establish
home industry, and will become somewhat more self-
sufficient, they must not develop as autarchies. Their
experience with dependence on world trade has not been
happy, and it would be understandable if they were to
press for making themselves economically as independent
of the rest of the world as possible. They can be persuaded
that their own rapid growth requires that their development
be based on a considerable international division of labor.
If we and they follow trade and monetary policies designed
to restore an effective international trading community,
and if their investment programs are consciously designed
to exploit their international comparative advantage, not
only will we and they benefit, but the other industrialized
nations, especially in Western Europe, will be able to
maintain rates of economic growth they would otherwise

have difficulty supporting. This is explained at greater
length in Chapter 8.

The Productive Use of Agricultural Surpluses

Second, there is a resource which, with a little intelligent
planning, could be made to play a much more important
part in international efforts to promote development than
it has done to date. This is the large agricultural surplus
of the United States and the other agricultural exporting
nations. Development is still inhibited in a number of
areas of the world for lack of an assured supply of food
and fibers, while in other areas an excess of agricultural
production continues to be an embarrassment. Chapter 9
suggests ways in which this paradox could be resolved to
the mutual benefit of both sets of countries.

7 CRITERIA OF ELIGIBILITY FOR ASSISTANCE

Four Banking Standards

WE HAVE EMPHASIZED THAT capital should be made available only where there is reasonable assurance that it will be productively used. Indeed, our central idea—that funds be allocated according to a banking concept of credit worthiness and technical absorptive capacity—hinges on the possibility of establishing criteria sufficiently objective that experts could readily determine whether a given application of resources was likely to justify itself in terms of increased productivity. While the element of judgment will always be important, of course, as it is in any banking operation, we believe it is possible to set forth with considerable precision the considerations on which judgment must be based.

At least four kinds of considerations must be involved:

A. It must be within the technical and administrative capabilities of the receiving country to carry out its proposed project with reasonable efficiency, over the time period of the loan or grant.

B. Steps must have been taken to insure that the rest of the economy of the receiving country is being developed sufficiently to make the proposed project fully productive in the time period envisaged by the loan.

C. The receiving country must have an over-all national development program designed to make the most effective possible use of its resources; this should include not only a series of interrelated capital projects but also necessary educational and training programs.

D. The receiving country's national development program must be consistent with the requirements of expanding world commerce and the international division of labor.

Management

Each of these criteria deserves explanation. The first is for the most part of a kind that any lending organization would automatically apply. Are there trained managers to run the project? Is adequately skilled labor available? Has provision been made to insure competent technical supervision? Any investment banker could spell out these requirements in detail. The application of these rather simple criteria will probably exclude in the first instance a large proportion of the proposals of the underdeveloped areas; but lending agencies should not confine themselves to ruling that the criteria have not been met. An essential part of our proposal is that lending agencies would provide advice and assistance to make good the deficiencies discovered. They would do this directly themselves, or they would refer the case to the national or international agencies specifically responsible for supplying technical assistance.

Balance

The second criterion is likewise one that lending agencies customarily apply. Do markets exist or can they be foreseen for the product of proposed installations? Are transport, communications, and public services adequate to serve the needs of the project, or will they be developed in time to do so? Have complementary activities producing the materials and services needed by the proposed project been planned on the required scale? Again, rejection of project applications because of failure to meet this second criterion would be accompanied by recommendations for action to eliminate the deficiency.

The Case for Over-all National Development Programs

These two are frequently the only criteria applied in international investment operations. But, while important, they are much less important in a program of the scale here contemplated than the remaining two criteria. Let us look, therefore, in some detail at the requirement that the receiving country have a correctly designed over-all national development program.

For any substantial expansion of international investment above existing levels it is essential that investment *programs* (not merely projects) be developed by the receiving countries. Such programs are necessary to insure: (1) that the various component projects interrelate and reinforce each other; (2) that the general objectives implied in the entire pattern of projects are ones which the people of the country will support; (3) that the collection of projects and measures undertaken will produce a faster growth of national product than any other which is consistent with the goals of the society; (4) that the resources of the economy have been tapped for the maximum contribution they can make to its development; and (5) that foreign exchange requirements have been minimized.

Such programs should include both the investment planned by public authorities and some estimate of what can reasonably be expected from the private sector. In other words, they should project forward for a reasonable period the total pattern of investment for the entire economy, together with estimates of the sources from which resources for investment, both public and private, can be secured. Whether the economic philosophy of the country calls for close regulation of private investment or permits private capital very freely to seek its own outlets, some estimate of the pattern of private investment is essential to the planning of whatever supporting public activity is contemplated. The need for programming derives from the fact that, in the transition stage of development, the success of many particular investment projects depends upon the entire set of investments being undertaken simultaneously.

At the least, the existence of such a national development program is evidence that the country has explicitly faced certain fundamental choices about its development—such as the relative weight to be given to agriculture as against industry; the fraction of resources to be devoted to social overhead capital such as railroads or public utilities and the like; the importance to be placed on consumers' capital (like housing) as against more directly productive instruments. A national program will naturally reflect the values and goals of the people of the country for which it is drawn. The purpose of review by an agency outside the country is not to pass on those values but to insure the program's internal consistency, to make certain that all relevant issues have been faced, and, where the program rests strictly on economic or technical relations, to see that they have been correctly applied.

An important consideration must be the adequacy of the measures undertaken by the country to capture the maximum flow of savings from its own citizens. The financial mechanism and the tax structure must be so designed as to eliminate pockets of either unemployed or misapplied resources. Savings channels must be set up to maximize the flow of savings, both small and large, into developmental investment. Fiscal management must be so designed as to prevent unhealthy inflation. All of these criteria are capable of generating frictions and differences of view between supplying and receiving countries. They must, of course, be applied in a wise and realistic manner with an understanding of what is politically and administratively possible in the particular country in question. But we believe frictions can be minimized and understanding and agreement promoted by the international adoption of a code such as is suggested in a later section.

There are few countries which will be able to meet this third criterion while in the first stage of growth. Nevertheless, investment can go forward on the basis of the first two criteria where it is clear that the particular project in question will be part of any sensible national development program, whatever its details. Many investments in transportation, public services, basic power sources, and improvement of agricultural techniques will be of this character. Thus, some loans or grants could probably be approved on a project basis in the absence of a national program; but before the levels of investment contemplated in our proposal can be reached, many underdeveloped countries must institute much more sophisticated programming procedures than they now have. Indeed, in most cases it will be impossible to pass on the soundness of an individual project, even according to conventional investors' standards, without familiarity with the national program of which it is a part. In a developed economy the environment of a project often changes slowly enough to be taken as given. In an economy undergoing sudden transition everything changes together, and the whole pattern of change must be examined to evaluate any part. Agencies applying this third criterion to investment projects can be of great help in assisting countries to undertake effective national programming.

One criterion in particular which the private banker customarily employs must give way to this broader criterion of contribution to a consistent national program. Private loans often hang on the question of whether the project to be financed is self-liquidating in the sense that its operation will directly produce the revenues necessary to repay the loan. This is a very poor criterion for development loans. A project may be self-liquidating because it discourages other investments which would otherwise take place and attracts to itself revenues which constitute a diversion rather than an increase of total product. On the other hand, a project such as an irrigation scheme may greatly expand total output but may be of such a character that it is not possible to collect equivalent added revenue from the immediate beneficiaries.

All projects taken together, that is, the whole national effort, should be self-liquidating in the sense that the national product created over time exceeds the national cost incurred. Moreover, each individual project should clearly produce over time a sufficient increase in the total product of the country to more than cover the costs of interest and amortization of the capital it requires. For example, the increase may take the form of lower costs to other industries, and need not accrue in an identifiable way to the project. The narrow criterion of whether a project can repay from its own revenues is at best irrelevant and may at worst be seriously misleading.

Generating Foreign Exchange

A distinction must be made between the productivity of an investment in creating new output within the country where it is made and its productivity in creating foreign exchange earnings out of which foreign borrowings can be repaid. It seldom makes sense to apply the test of foreign-exchange earning power to particular projects. The possibilities of repayment of a foreign loan will depend on the entire balance of payments position of the borrowing country at the time interest and amortization payments fall due. The risk of foreign-exchange difficulties in the period of repayment is greatest for a country in the first or precondition stage, less in the second stage, and least in the third or self-sustaining stage. This is true partly because as development proceeds the economy becomes more diversified and flexible, and its opportunities of production for foreign markets grow; and partly because, as development becomes regularized, it can more easily attract new capital to replace that being withdrawn. This constitutes an added reason for supplying a good part of the limited amounts of capital needed in the first stage in the form of grants, soft loans with local currency repayment, or equities which can be recovered only if the economy in fact moves into the transition.

Whether foreign-exchange difficulties will be encountered in the second and third stages depends partly on the kind of international trading environment which has been established by that time. This in turn depends partly on the adoption of our fourth criterion: that countries pay attention to the possibilities of the international division of labor. We turn to this problem in the next chapter.

8 THE INTERNATIONAL DIVISION OF LABOR

How Autarchy Arises

THE FOURTH CRITERION WOULD
seek to insure that the national development programs exploit the possibilities of international division of labor, foster international trade, and avoid extreme autarchy. This criterion deserves special attention, since its observance is important not only to the underdeveloped countries but also to the economies of the industrialized countries, including the United States. It is, moreover, a criterion on which the United States cannot insist unless we are prepared to set an example by modifying our own trade policies so as more nearly to conform with its requirements.

Officials in the underdeveloped countries, understandably preoccupied with internal problems, may well fail to pay adequate attention to the ways in which their own economies can gain from being integrated into an expanding world economy. In a stable world of free trading relations such as are sometimes mistakenly thought to have characterized the nineteenth century, the development program for any country which produced the largest internal rate of growth would also be the one which took most advantage of the possibilities of international specialization and division of labor. But in the contemporary unstable world, plagued by extreme fluctuations in the prices of basic commodities, subject to almost daily changes in the terms and conditions on which international trade is carried on, and, above all, subject to the overriding risk that foreign areas may be cut off altogether at almost any moment by political or military developments, programming authorities are under great pressure to abandon the obvious benefits of international trade for the security of some degree of autarchy.

This results in decisions of two sorts. In the first place, some underdeveloped countries are slow to see and to give priority to opportunities to invest in the production of things that could be sold abroad. Many countries still possess undeveloped mineral and raw-material resources which could be further exploited to provide the supplies needed by the industries of Japan, Western Europe, and the United States. But partly because extractive industry has been associated with colonialism and partly because international markets have been unreliable, underdeveloped countries have frequently been reluctant to give serious consideration to investments of this sort. Beyond this there are possibilities of specialization as among the underdeveloped countries themselves which have not been considered because development planning in each country has stopped at its own borders.

In the second place some countries, partly through tariffs and quotas and partly through exchange controls, have imposed severe restrictions on the import of many kinds of goods in the hope that they could develop efficient production of these things themselves under an umbrella of protection. Some of these restrictions are justified. Where internal taxation procedures have not been adequately developed, import duties have been one of the few effective ways of restricting the luxury consumption of the very wealthy classes. Economists have long recognized that there is some validity to the infant-industry argument for protection in a young country. Indeed, American industry was given its start behind tariff barriers on just such grounds. Industries must attain a certain scale and acquire a certain level of experience before they can hope to reduce their costs to the level of large established competitors abroad. Without some initial protection competitive industries often cannot get started. Nevertheless, it would be hard to contend that all the trade restrictions applied by the underdeveloped countries could be justified on rational grounds.

Tempering Tendencies Toward Autarchy

In the interests of maximizing productivity in the underdeveloped countries, a new program of capital assistance to development should contain safeguards against an exaggerated trend toward autarchy. The economic costs of attempted self-sufficiency in some industries in which the underdeveloped countries have no experience or natural advantage would probably be great enough to frustrate the possibility of over-all growth; for many of them are comparatively small countries with markets inadequate, both now and in the foreseeable future, to support many industries requiring large-scale operation. Although diversification is a reasonable goal for an economy, it makes no economic sense to push it to the extreme of attempted self-sufficiency—especially in a small economy.

More positively, there are substantial possibilities that economies could result from regional co-operation in investment plans. Through such co-operation each country could devote a special investment effort to enterprises in which it had comparative advantages, secure in the expectation of sales larger than its domestic market could justify. Indonesia, with cheap natural gas, might export fertilizer to the whole South Asian area, India might be a source of light engineering, and so on. This would require discussion and, possibly, long-term agreements among the programming authorities of the various countries of a region; but it might yield big dividends in productivity for all the participants.

The Interest of the Industrialized Nations

Important reasons for promoting the international division of labor arise also from the requirements of the industrialized nations. They no longer face a shortage of resources for self-sustained economic development, but they do face a continuing problem of adjustment to the international economy. The proposal made in this book could help substantially to solve their chronic trade problems.

The economies of the industrialized nations developed in an era of international specialization and international trade; and without continued specialization and trade they certainly cannot provide expanding incomes for their people and may not be able even to maintain their present standards of living. They need two things: expanding markets in which they can sell those goods they can produce most cheaply, and expanding sources for food and raw materials which they cannot efficiently produce at home. Without a restoration of international trade there is little hope of finding a solution for the growth problems of the developed countries of Western Europe and Japan.

At the moment, the international position of the Western European countries appears to have improved. Most of them have succeeded in increasing their reserves of foreign exchange, and the gap between black-market exchange rates and official rates has narrowed in many instances. However, it should be kept in mind that the total flow of aid, military and economic, has not been going down in the last few years. The impact of a sharp reduction in this flow, with no change in the burden of their own military expenditure, would be serious. Furthermore, expanding levels of income in Europe will require expanding levels of trade, because greater production in Europe requires both greater imports of materials and the stimulus of expanded markets. The Japanese situation is much more serious. Japan has been able to maintain her level of activity only because of the extraordinary disbursements of the United States in Japan connected with the Korean War and its aftermath. The Japanese economy, the prewar prosperity of which was built on trade, needs a trade revival merely to survive, let alone to grow.

In the short run it would be foolish to exaggerate the economic importance for the developed countries of access to the materials and markets of the underdeveloped areas. The flow of raw materials from Asia, Africa, and Latin America is not going to be abruptly interrupted, and trade among the industrial countries themselves has always been more important to each of them than trade with low-income areas. Nonetheless, as time goes on, the policies of the underdeveloped areas can become increasingly critical to the small margin of trade opportunities which makes the difference between growth and stagnation in Europe and Japan. If investment in extractive industries for export stops or falls off sharply in each area as it achieves independence from colonial rule, raw-material costs will rise and countries dependent upon imported materials will suffer with no corresponding advantage to the exporting area. If, on the other hand, some part of the capital resources of the underdeveloped countries continues to be devoted to reducing the costs of raw-material exports, their short-run foreign-exchange position will be improved, and in the long run their own growing economies will benefit from lower-cost domestic raw materials. This is not an argument against desirable diversification but rather against a complete neglect of export industries in investment programs. It may be possible through such devices as long-term purchase agreements to reduce somewhat the violence of fluctuations in raw-material export prices, and it should be a firm objective of the underdeveloped areas progressively to increase the extent to which they themselves process their own raw materials before export.

So far as markets are concerned, in the short run the process of development itself generates requirements for capital goods and equipment which can provide an important outlet for European and Japanese manufactures. Some of these sales can be financed by the capital contributions that developed countries other than the United States can make to development programs. But the capacity of Western Europe and Japan to finance their own exports has narrow limits. This circumstance places a special responsibility on the United States. Dollars supplied to the underdeveloped countries by the United States could do double duty if we do not attach "buy American" strings to our loans and grants. Some portion of our dollar contribution to development spent in Europe and Japan for capital equipment will strengthen the dollar-buying power of these countries and thus indirectly stimulate our own exports. Thus, if we do not restrict its spending to this country, the American development assistance contribution can become an important lubricant of international trade everywhere and hasten the day when currency and trade restrictions growing out of the postwar dollar shortage can be done away with.

In the longer run, as the underdeveloped countries develop and become industrialized, their participation in world trade can become quantitatively much more important to total world-trade flows. Fears that as they develop they will become competitors of presently industrialized countries and thus reduce export opportunities should be quieted by the history of industrialization. As standards of living rise in a country, the growth in the magnitude and variety of its demands much more than compensates as a rule for such reduction as occurs in those limited types of imports it now produces at home. The trade possibilities opened up when the incomes of several hundred million people expand from fifty dollars per year per head to four or six or ten times that amount are almost impossible to visualize.

An American Responsibility

Whether or not these bright hopes come to pass depends in considerable degree, of course, on American commercial policy. It is very much in our interest that the underdeveloped countries themselves earn through export to dollar areas as large a part of the resources needed for their development as possible. They will not earn much in the immediate future. As their economies grow, however, they should be increasingly able to compete effectively in U.S. markets if our tariff policies do not prevent them from doing so. In the long run our development loans can be repaid only if they or their customers can so compete.

Second, the lubricating effect on international trade of a flow of development dollars from this country will depend entirely on our not thwarting that effect by insisting that the dollars be immediately spent in this country. The pressures to maintain "buy American" provisions will be strong from particular export interests. The national interest, and even the longer-run export interest of the United States, will be much better served if those pressures are resisted.

Perhaps more important than either of these considerations, however, is the force of our example. If the United States, the strongest, most self-sufficient economy in the world, is not prepared to open its economy to legitimate foreign competition, we can hardly expect that our admonitions to the rest of the world to abide by the principles of free trade will be received with good grace. We certainly cannot insist on an acceptance of the principle of international division of labor as a criterion for eligibility for development assistance unless we are prepared to abide by that principle ourselves. And it will be increasingly to our own economic as well as political interest to have that principle accepted elsewhere as time goes by.

Creating the Conditions for Convertibility

A word must be said about the relation of our proposal to the problem of general Free World convertibility of currencies. We do not believe that the institution of convertibility will, by itself, do much to solve the underlying problems of the industrialized countries, let alone the underdeveloped ones. Convertibility can be achieved only if the underlying conditions for it exist. A commitment by the United States and other dollar areas, however, to provide the world's trading system with a substantial increment of dollars for development programs which meet the criteria of efficient international specialization might well make Free World convertibility a workable arrangement, provided that a substantial part of the dollar grants and loans is not tied to dollar purchases. We are convinced that the desire for convertibility is strong and general enough to bring it about once confidence in the scale and stability of U.S. action is established. Such confidence can be produced by U.S. willingness to proceed with these proposals. It cannot be produced by diplomatic pressure.

9   THE ROLE OF AGRICULTURAL SURPLUSES

Putting Surpluses to Work

WE BELIEVE THAT IN THE context of our proposal arrangements could be worked out for the use of very much larger quantities of foods and fibers in development programs than have been utilized to date—and without disrupting international commodity markets or interfering with the sale of foods and fibers in those markets by other exporting nations. The underdeveloped countries need a program designed not merely to supply capital goods or other items available only from abroad but also to expand their general resources in all ways which will promote domestic capital formation.

Many of the underdeveloped countries have a huge unemployed or underemployed labor force which could be used for developmental purposes. In most of the Asian countries there are many people now idle or ineffectively employed whose labor, once mobilized, could build roads, houses, factories, canals, and irrigation works, reclaim land, and modernize villages.

There is a negative as well as a positive case for putting this underemployed labor to work.

If not given employment, these men, increasingly intent on improving their lot, could constitute a serious political problem. India, for example, in spite of a quite ambitious second five-year plan, does not now expect to be able to reduce her large volume of unemployment significantly over the next five years, since new employment opportunities will barely match increases in her labor force resulting from population growth.

Why Labor Is Underemployed

Three obstacles stand in the way of utilizing this pool of underemployed labor. The first is a scarcity of administrative and managerial talent to supervise projects on which this labor could be employed. This situation is slowly being improved both by the efforts of the countries themselves and by the international technical assistance programs operating within them. The second obstacle is the lack of the minimum amounts of capital equipment required to undertake even the most labor-intensive types of projects. This shortage could be largely overcome by procedures already discussed as part of the program proposed in this book. The third obstacle is that the unemployed are underfed and underclothed. It is this third obstacle with which we are concerned here.

If the unemployed are put to work at wages supplied by the government, they will spend those wages largely on additional food and clothing. If there is not sufficient additional food and clothing available, the increased demand will push up the prices of these essential articles, and general inflation will result. Therefore, the volume of wage payments which the authorities of the underdeveloped countries feel they can safely undertake is limited by their estimate of the likelihood that such payments will indirectly push up prices, especially the prices of essentials. However, their estimate of the risks of inflation is complicated by the uncertainties of the weather. An undertaking which would be safe if the season turned out to be favorable might produce disastrous inflation if there were a bad harvest. Storage facilities in the underdeveloped countries are in general most inadequate, and there is thus no way for them to build up adequate stocks for emergencies.

A Specific Proposal

We propose, therefore, that there be established an international food and fiber bank on which the underdeveloped countries could draw. If additional capital were provided along the lines of our general proposal, these countries would and could draw on the food and fiber bank to implement plans to employ productively a considerably greater part of their presently idle labor force. Demands on the food and fiber bank would, we believe, be substantial. Since it takes time and scarce resources to organize labor-intensive projects, and since, once started, they cannot easily be discontinued at short notice, favorable results could be expected only if assurance were given that both the capital and the food and fiber supplies would be available over a considerable period of time. Therefore, the horizon of an international food and fiber program should be at least five and preferably ten years.

A warning is necessary here. Where the other two conditions are not met—organizing skill and minimum capital equipment—the movement of agricultural commodities into the markets of underdeveloped countries can have damaging effects. For if there is an increase in agricultural supplies without any corresponding increase in demand, agricultural prices may fall sharply, reducing the incomes of peasants and slowing or stopping programs of agricultural and village improvement. Furthermore, some of the underdeveloped countries which export agricultural surpluses depend on the sale of such surpluses for the imports which they, in turn, require for their own development. Thus the unplanned dumping abroad of agricultural surpluses can be much worse than useless. It can be disastrous.

Meshing with Commercial Markets

A program for the use of agricultural surpluses must have several features if it is to avoid interfering with the normal marketing of agricultural products both within the receiving countries and by the exporting nations. In the first place, countries should be assured that they could draw on food and fiber supplies if necessary to meet expanding demands or abnormally short supplies, but that they would be under no obligation to take such supplies if domestic supplies and normal imports were adequate. The pragmatic test would probably be the behavior of prices of food and fiber. Indeed, to protect the exporting countries, the program should probably contain a provision that no country would be permitted to draw on the stocks in the international food and fiber bank unless prices in its domestic markets rose above certain normal levels.

A second protection for the exporting countries would be that they would themselves be invited to participate in supplying commodities to the international food and fiber bank on a basis determined by their normal shares in international commodity movements. Exporting countries like Canada which are suppliers of developmental capital for the underdeveloped countries would be encouraged to make their contribution partly in agricultural commodities. Exporting countries like Burma, which are in need of developmental assistance, would receive such assistance partly in the form of purchases of Burmese rice for the food bank with hard currencies which Burma could use for developmental purposes.

This food and fiber program looks on the face of it very like a number of international commodity stabilization schemes which have been put forward in the past. It differs from them in that, by providing assurances that food and fiber would be available to prevent expenditure from having inflationary effects, it would encourage countries to undertake local developmental expenditure. As to payment, the food bank should probably accept at least in the early stages local currency which would be held in a counterpart funds account. This fund could be used as part of the capital-supply program of the developed countries, or, if the monetary situation required, it could be held idle as a damper to inflation.

How Much of the Job Can Surpluses Do?

Experts who have studied the problem in the full light of these considerations are convinced that, in a development program which also provides capital goods and which is planned for some years ahead in the light of the various bottlenecks existing in the economy of the recipient country, there are possibilities for the use of a very substantial volume of agricultural commodities in assistance programs. The FAO, for instance, has estimated that something like 100 million dollars' worth of agricultural surpluses could be used annually in India in connection with an expansion of 250 million dollars per year in India's investment program. In general it appears that from 15 per cent to 25 per cent of all foreign capital required by all underdeveloped countries could take the form of agricultural commodities.

If this estimate is correct, and the estimate of total capital requirements given in the next chapter is reasonable, agricultural surpluses could be used to the extent of around 500 million dollars' worth per year over and above extraordinary relief requirements in exceptionally bad crop years. Various ideas have been put forward for distributing more food through channels entirely outside the market mechanism, like school lunch programs and special free meals for project workers. In our view such schemes are likely to be both inefficient and quantitatively limited. Some such program as we propose for food and fiber stocks to provide insurance against the inflationary consequences of additional wage payments offers more hope for substantial use of agricultural surpluses in development efforts. The program will be more effective, of course, the larger the number of essential commodities which can be included in the reserves.

10   THE MAGNITUDE OF CAPITAL REQUIREMENTS

What Determines the Price Tag

PRECEDING CHAPTERS HAVE outlined our proposal that the developed countries of the world should undertake, through a variety of channels, to make available to the underdeveloped countries sufficient capital to meet all requests which satisfy certain criteria. This proposal at once raises three questions: (1) If this offer were made, what is the *maximum* amount which might have to be provided annually to make good on it? (2) What are the chances that this amount would be sufficient to set in motion a process of self-sustaining growth in the underdeveloped areas? (3) What is the *probable* level of eligible requests over the next five to ten years?

Several factors limit the volume of capital assistance

95

that the underdeveloped countries are likely to be in a position to absorb productively. A limit on the size of a national development program and on the number of desirable and feasible projects is set by the ability of the underdeveloped country to organize, administer, and carry out projects and to relate them to one another in such a way that the output of each project is used productively. Foreign technical assistance and advice can raise this limit somewhat, particularly in certain specialized types of projects. The countries themselves, however, are reluctant to turn over project management and control too largely to foreign experts; and, even if they were not politically sensitive on this point, it is doubtful that their own long-run development would be effectively promoted by enterprises for which they do not take a share of responsibility.

It is extremely hazardous to attempt to estimate technical absorptive capacity. It will vary widely from country to country, depending partly on a country's state of development and partly on its history and traditions. We believe, however, that it is reasonable to assume that the average maximum expansion in the level of capital formation that can be achieved by countries in the early stages of development is from 30 to 50 per cent in the first three or four years after planning for such expansion is initiated. There will be some instances in which even this is too high a figure, and others in which a single project like a dam or an irrigation system may involve expenditures exceeding this limit. However, an examination of existing national programs gives us some confidence that this is a reasonable order of magnitude.

It is most unlikely that countries in the very early stages of development can find sufficient resources within their own economies to make more than a very small contribution to such an expanded level of investment. Since their populations are at the margin of subsistence, consumption cannot be reduced in order to free resources for investment. Furthermore, their relatively primitive methods of mobilizing such savings as they can generate are unlikely to tap more than a fraction of these. There are certain countries, notably those producing oil, in which the revenue from an exportable resource provides the means for development expenditure without cuts in consumption by the population as a whole, but these cases do not bulk large in the total of capital requirements for development. Accordingly, it seems reasonable to assume that for countries in the precondition stage of development virtually all of the additional capital needed to launch the growth process must be supplied from outside.

Once the growth process is under way, two things happen which affect the need for external capital in opposite ways. In the first place, the capacity of the country to absorb capital rises rapidly. A trained class of administrators appears; skilled labor is increasingly available; transport, power, and communications are increasingly able to fill the needs of new enterprises; markets are expanding; and the motivations required to stimulate innovation, risk-taking, and efficiency progressively develop. At the same time, as income rises, a portion of each year's income can be plowed back in further investment, and the society becomes increasingly capable of mobilizing this fraction for development. The fraction of this *increase* in income which can be saved is much larger than the fraction of *total* income which can be saved. Although in Asia, for instance, the *average* rate of savings from *total* income is probably not much above 5 per cent, the rate of saving from *increases* in income can be pushed as high as 20 to 25 or even 30 per cent. Thus, at the same time that the absorptive capacity of the economy rises, its capacity to supply its own capital needs out of its own resources also rises. If additional external capital is supplied at an annual rate of something like 30 to 50 per cent of the rates of investment prevailing in a country at the beginning of the development process, the country can mobilize sufficient saving out of the increases in its income to keep pace with its own growing capacity to use capital. Indeed, once the take-off occurs—that is, once a regular rate of growth in national income has begun—the requirement for a net inflow of foreign capital on a substantial scale is unlikely to last for more than ten or fifteen years. After that period of time the country can put itself in a position to supply all of its own requirements out of its own resources. It may still attract foreign capital, but it can do so on terms attractive to private international investors.

Some Rough Figures

To estimate, then, the amounts of foreign capital that could productively be absorbed by the underdeveloped countries, one must consider countries in two categories. First, for those which have not yet entered into the transition stage of growing national income the estimate can be made by taking 30 to 50 per cent of present levels of capital formation. For those which have begun to grow the percentage will be less, being the smallest for those farthest along in the growth process. These estimates, explained in greater detail in the Appendix, result in the following figures:

	Billions of Dollars Per Year
India, Pakistan, Ceylon	0.8–1.0
Balance of non-Communist Asia (excluding Japan)	0.4–0.6
Middle East (excluding Pakistan but including Egypt)	0.3–0.5
Latin America	0.8–1.0
Africa (excluding Egypt and Union of South Africa)	0.2–0.4
TOTAL	2.5–3.5

Since our purpose was to estimate the maximum amounts of foreign capital which underdeveloped countries could use productively, we must take the higher end of the range as our figure for planning purposes, recognizing that actual demands are likely to be somewhat lower.

Our second question is whether levels of investment of the magnitude suggested in this table would be sufficient to launch the underdeveloped areas into a period of growing per capita levels of income. Computations are given in the Appendix which suggest that these levels of capital formation should produce rates of growth of per capita incomes of at least 1 or 2 per cent per year. The procedure used in this demonstration is roughly as follows: starting with estimates of the national incomes of all the under-developed areas, one can make estimates of the capital-output ratio which may apply in each region; that is, of the number of units of capital required to produce an increase of one unit per year in output. The capital-output ratio used in these computations was 3:1. This is believed to be a conservative—that is, a high—figure. The figure used in the Indian second five-year plan, for example, is about 2.3:1.

Applying this capital-output ratio to the levels of total investment which would obtain in the underdeveloped areas if the amounts of capital in the above table were supplied from foreign sources, one gets rates of growth of national income ranging from 2.5 to 4 per cent. Since population growth ranges from 1.5 to 2 per cent in most of the underdeveloped areas, the resulting per capita rates of growth of income are from 1 to 2 per cent per year. In countries already launched on the growth process, which will be making increasing contributions to capital formation annually out of their own resources, the rates of growth of per capita income may be somewhat higher.

India illustrates the general principles set forth above. Foreign capital requirements for India included in the above table represent over 50 per cent of the level of net capital formation achieved in India in 1953. India's second five-year plan, beginning this year, calls for a much higher level of capital formation than in recent years. However, because India's national income has begun to grow, the proportion of her capital requirements that she can meet out of her own resources has also begun to grow. Her requirement for foreign capital for the second plan represents, therefore, less than 20 per cent of the investment programmed for the whole five-year period.

The figure of 3.5 billion dollars arrived at above assumes that every country confronted with the possibility of securing whatever capital it can productively use will within two or three years be able to submit acceptable programs and projects which would utilize 30 to 50 per cent more capital than it has been investing in the recent past. At first, of course, the flow would be much less than the suggested figure. But we assume that, if a standing commitment to finance well-designed national programs up to a given limit were announced and maintained, what is called technical absorptive capacity *could* be stepped up on the average by about 40 per cent within about three years. Very few governments will make the effort of preparing national investment programs for which no resources are in sight, but once the assurance is given that capital will be forthcoming, their programming effort will increase considerably. We asume that, after the announcement of the program we propose, roughly two years might be required for the elaboration of well-prepared national programs and projects, and perhaps a third year for solving the problem of logistics (selecting proper equipment, purchasing organizations, etc.).

Thus, if all countries were equally efficient at working out acceptable national programs and projects, a commitment made today of a target amount of annual aid should lead to disbursements beginning on a large scale only after about three years. If by this process absorptive capacity were increased by 30-50 per cent, the amount of foreign investment called for would be, at a maximum, about 3.5 billion per annum. This amount would make possible a rise in per capita output of at least 1 or 2 per cent per year. Technical absorptive capacity would continue to rise after the first three years by 5 to 10 per cent per year, but the additional capital required to take advantage of this rise could be supplied from domestic savings.

In practice, the rate at which countries will be able to qualify for capital will vary according to their stage of development. Some countries are probably prepared right now to absorb productively substantial additional sums (e.g., India); some might organize themselves to use sizable amounts in a few years (e.g., Indonesia); some may require a decade or more before the preconditions for effective investment on any scale are established (e.g., certain African regions). Thus it seems most unlikely that, if a commitment to make available 3.5 billion dollars annually is entered into, the rate of actual disbursement will rise above, say, 60 per cent of that amount. Thus, on the average, we would predict an annual actual flow, once the program got going, of something like two billion dollars.

It should be emphasized, however, that, if such a pro-

gram as we envisage is to exert real pressure, the commitment must be greater than expected disbursements. If the
commitment is pared below the above suggested figure,
the actual disbursements will also fall at least in proportion.
We regard it as of the highest importance that sums of
the full order of magnitude suggested above be offered
to insure that capital is forthcoming whenever clear
criteria for productive investment are met.

Where the Money Might Come from

The maximum figure of 3.5 billion dollars refers to the
total annual additional foreign capital inflow into the underdeveloped areas from all sources. Present capital inflows
constitute part of the base on which the 30 to 50 per cent
addition was computed. Thus the 3.5 billion dollar figure
is in addition to what is now flowing. It should be noted
that the net capital flow abroad from the United States to
the underdeveloped areas outside Latin America has been
quite small. Only a very small fraction of the U.S. aid
program has been devoted to capital for developmental
purposes. The bulk of it has been either direct military
assistance, general assistance to current budgets to permit
recipient countries to maintain a large military establishment, or relief and rehabilitation in such areas as South
Korea and South Vietnam. In Latin America there has
been a good deal of American private investment, but it
has been offset to a considerable degree by current amortization payments on foreign debts by the Latin American
countries. Well over half the capital inflow currently going

to the underdeveloped areas represents the provision of capital by the European countries to their dependent overseas territories.

It is difficult to be precise about the breakdown of the 3.5 billion dollars by sources of supply. Under appropriate conditions there is room for a substantial expansion of private investment. Against the background of the intergovernmental effort envisaged, it is believed that over time major progress might be made in increasing the flow of private capital to the underdeveloped areas. Changes in the U.S. revenue code may help encourage more direct investment, as would a revitalization of the transfer guarantee by the Export-Import Bank. The recently established International Finance Corporation (IFC), affiliated with the International Bank, is a hopeful device for encouraging the participation of private capital in international ventures. We would support the development of similar institutions, such as the Indian Development Corporation, within receiving countries.

Since successful private investment projects generally require a favorable environment in terms of expanding local markets, available transport and communication facilities, and the like, their share in the early stages of development must necessarily be low. Public loans, by helping to create the necessary environment, can pave the way for greatly expanded private investment as growth takes hold. We should not set our hopes for private investment flows too high, too soon; but the effort to expand these flows should be pushed promptly, with vigor.

The lack of success hitherto achieved in negotiating a more favorable climate for private investment should not be taken as evidence that further efforts will be futile. International private-capital flows have been held up partly by insufficient availability of public credit and partly by political and psychological blocks which have already perceptively diminished, although they have by no means disappeared. In the context of the program we propose it may well be appropriate for the international development agency proposed in Chapter 11 to draw up a Free World code for private capital movements which would incorporate the best lessons of recent experience in protecting both the national sovereignty of the recipient and the legitimate economic interest of the lender.

The International Bank could step up its lending rate substantially if new projects were eligible under its rules. Its resources for carrying on such operations could be expanded by additional sales of its securities in the U.S. bond market.

Of the remainder to be supplied through public channels, it is certainly desirable that a portion should come from other developed countries. Europe has expanded its own economic base enough since the war to make a significant additional contribution. In our judgment, the importance of generating substantial capital commitments from the well-developed countries of the Free World other than the United States cannot be overestimated. Joint creation of capital funds not only will make the concept of partnership more persuasive in the United

States; it is also essential in order to impart to the enterprise the international character requisite for its acceptance and continued support in the underdeveloped areas.

The problem of what proportion should be loans and what proportion grants is also complex. Grants would be appropriate primarily to countries at the earliest stage of development where the prediction of repayment capability is the most hazardous, and credit-worthiness is limited. Since these will be the countries with the lowest technical absorptive capacity, it is reasonable to assume that grants would be a quite small part of the total estimated 3.5 billion dollars.

On the basis of these considerations the supply of the maximum annual figure of 3.5 billion dollars might break down by source as follows:

Grants:	
U.S. contribution	$ 360 million
Other country contribution	240
Direct Private Investment	500
Additional International Bank Loans	400
Public Loans:	
U.S. contribution	1,700
Other country contribution	300
TOTAL	$3,500 million

The American Contribution

Thus the *maximum* burden of our proposed program on the U.S. Treasury would be about two billion dollars per year, of which over 80 per cent would be loans. This sum would almost certainly never actually be reached. It is based on maximum estimates of the absorptive capacity of the recipient countries, on the assumption that they do, everything within their power to increase that capacity. Actual demands for the first two or three years would be much smaller than this; and, because some countries will be much slower to develop absorptive capacity than others, the rate of withdrawals is unlikely ever to exceed 60 per cent or so of this figure, or a U.S. government obligation of about 1.2 billion dollars per year.

In addition to the capital program, the level of U.S. technical assistance, offered either directly or through the United Nations, should probably be raised about 100 million dollars per year. Also, we have made no allowance here for the special needs of Japan. Although Japan had passed into the third or self-sustaining phase of development before World War II, that war not only exposed her to serious physical destruction but also, and more important, resulted in the necessity for a reorientation of her trade which has not yet been successfully accomplished. If all the measures advocated in this book were adopted, including the liberalization of trade restrictions and the supplying of capital without "buy American" strings, it would be our hope that the Japanese balance of payments problem could in the long run be largely solved. There will probably be a transitional period of five to ten years, however, during which loans of one or two hundred million dollars a year for Japan will be necessary. Taking all these things together, the total U.S. Treasury burden of a program such as is here advocated would not be likely to exceed 1.5 billion dollars; and this level would not be reached for several years, by which time the requirements for military assistance spending might have been somewhat reduced.

We must emphasize again, however, that while this is our best estimate of the amounts that would actually be drawn upon, it is an absolutely essential feature of this proposal that the amounts offered be sufficient to cover greater demands in the event that more countries should be more successful in increasing their capacity to use capital productively than we have assumed.

It is important to be crystal clear as to the economic purpose of the proposed loans and grants. They would not be designed to meet a requirement for foreign exchange or for particular goods which can be supplied only from abroad. They would be designed to supplement the over-all resources of the underdeveloped countries in order to permit them to add to their productive equipment at a rate faster than would be possible without such loans. They would be used for the import of such equipment itself or for the import, for example, of food to meet the higher demand resulting from greater employment in develop-mental activities. Indeed, as explained in Chapter 9, a significant part of the total U.S. contribution could be in agricultural surpluses. Criteria would be rigidly set to prevent the use of loans and grants for an unproductive and temporary expansion in consumption.

One requirement cannot be shirked if the program is

to succeed. The United States must discover a device for guaranteeing a continuity in capital loans and grants which would avoid an annual Congressional renewal of the effort. Without a firm conviction that the American portion of the effort will be sustained, none of the larger benefits of the proposal can be envisaged. One possible device would be to appropriate the necessary funds in a once-for-all act, looking ahead, say, five years, leaving discretion for their release to the Executive Branch of the government, following broadly the technique of appropriation now used with respect to the Export-Import Bank.

On the tentative but not unreasonable criteria set out above, the U.S. government commitment in loans and grants might come to two billion dollars per annum, of which 1.2 billion dollars might be disbursed, on the average, if sound criteria for efficient use were applied. Thus, the initial Congressional appropriation, under the organizational principle set out above, might be ten billion dollars for allocation over a five-year period.

We believe that a program conceived on this scale, stabilized for a substantial future period, founded on an incentive system which would remove capital as a bottleneck and throw the burden of responsibility on the developing areas, would maximize the pace of economic growth in the Free World.

11 INSTITUTIONS TO CARRY OUT THE PROGRAM

The Multiple Sources of Supply

THERE HAS BEEN MUCH debate as to what new institutional machinery would be required to carry out an expanded program of development assistance such as is proposed in this book. Capital and technical assistance are now supplied through a variety of channels, national and international. Technical assistance is available to underdeveloped countries through such international organizations as the U.N. Technical Assistance Administration, the World Health Organization, the Food and Agriculture Organization, and the International Labor Office; through national organizations set up by the governments of the United States, the Soviet Union, and other countries; through nonprofit private organizations like the American Friends Service Committee and the Ford Foundation; and through private consulting firms. Development loans can be secured from the International Bank, the Export-Import Bank, some foreign governments, and private capital sources. Equity capital can be secured in a variety of forms from private sources and from the new International Finance Corporation. Grants and "soft" loans requiring payment only in local currencies or on special terms have been made by the U.S. International Cooperation Administration and by other governments; and agricultural surpluses have been supplied to underdeveloped countries under a variety of schemes.

In addition to these various sources of finance, there are other national and international organizations which study, discuss, and attempt to co-ordinate in various ways national development efforts. These include regional organizations like the Colombo Plan and the Organization of American States; U.N. agencies such as the Secretariat in New York, the Economic Commission for Asia and the Far East, the Economic Commission for Latin America, and the Economic Commission for Europe; and a variety of national and private bodies. Any proposal for additional machinery must take into account the existence of all of these present channels for supplying and co-ordinating capital and technical assistance for development. An expanded program could require either one or more new institutions, an expansion in the scale of activity of existing institutions, or some combination of the two.

Two Unfilled Gaps

There are two quite different reasons why some new machinery is needed to carry out this proposal. In the first place, there is need for more effective programming and co-ordination of development activities. If, as seems probable and desirable, financing for development continues to come from a variety of sources, both suppliers and recipients need some central place where they can turn for information about the total development effort of which their activities are a part. Suppliers need an objective evaluation of the development programs to which they are asked to contribute, an appraisal of need in the light of financing available from other sources, consultation with recipients and with other suppliers as to the criteria to be applied in judging applications for funds, and information as to progress being made on national programs. Recipients need information as to all the alternative sources of funds and the purposes for which it is appropriate to seek financing from each, assistance in working out a consistent program of financing from all sources, advice on how to prepare programs to meet the requirements of a variety of suppliers, and the like. We have emphasized earlier that for countries in the early stages of development it is particularly true that a judgment on the wisdom and prospects of success of any particular project depends on an appraisal of the entire pattern of development activities which a country is undertaking. Both suppliers and recipients need some one place where this total pattern can be examined and considered.

Secondly, apart from this programming function, some new machinery is undoubtedly needed to administer a portion of the additional funds which we propose should be made available. Existing institutions should carry as much of the load as their charters and terms of reference permit. The resources of the International Bank should be increased if necessary to permit it to meet all requests which meet the credit standards it will apply. Private sources, in co-operation with the International Finance Corporation, will take a growing share of the load as time goes on. But a substantial expansion will be needed in loans, and in grants and loans with more liberal terms than the International Bank can offer or for more risky ventures than it can finance. This additional financing could be handled through existing national agencies, through new national agencies, or through a new international agency. The most widely discussed international proposal is for a new body affiliated with the United Nations, known as the Special United Nations Fund for Economic Development (SUNFED). The proposal calls for a Council representing all members of the United Nations willing to join the Fund, an Executive Board of twelve elected by the Council, a Director General, and a staff. Administrative expenses of the Fund would be covered by levies on the members proportional to their contributions to the U.N. The resources of the Fund would consist of voluntary contributions by member governments. To receive assistance from the Fund, a country would have to be a member. The Fund would make grants and loans at rates of interest lower than those charged by the International Bank. It would distribute its resources for development purposes in response to applications from countries which could make a reasonable showing that their legitimate development needs could not be met from other existing sources.

National versus International Administration

The debate over whether the additional financing required should be provided mainly through such an international body or through bilateral arrangements between supplying and recipient countries has been heated. We do not believe the basic issues underlying this debate have been explored thoroughly enough to permit us to present any detailed blueprint of the ideal solution, but we believe there are six fundamental considerations which must be borne in mind in selecting machinery, whether it take the form of new institutions or the adaptation of existing institutions.

First, a development assistance program such as the one here proposed should be administered quite separately from programs with military or more narrowly political purposes. There is every reason to believe that the United States will wish to continue some program of military assistance and to grant continued economic aid to some allies on grounds different from those proposed here; for example, to South Korea, Formosa, and Southern Vietnam.

Such assistance should not be confused with a general program for economic growth in the underdeveloped areas of the Free World. A general program will not achieve its objectives unless the recipients are convinced that their foreign policy is in no way compromised by participation in the program and that administration of the program will be unaffected by short-run variation in the winds of international politics. This condition cannot be assured by the adoption of any particular institutional scheme. Unless the United States and the other supplying countries make up their minds that they genuinely want to engage in an expanded program and are willing to apply the nonpolitical criteria described in Chapter 7, no pressure for the use of SUNFED or other international machinery will be of any avail. An international program on the required scale cannot be established without wholehearted U.S. participation. This will not be forthcoming unless the U.S. has first accepted the basic principles outlined in this book. Once it has accepted those principles, they can be successfully applied by either national or international agencies.

Second, there is great virtue in conducting a program of this kind in a spirit of partnership, both among the supplying countries and between them and the recipients. This is important first to avoid any suggestion of imperialist domination; second to avoid invidious distinctions between grantor and grantee countres; and third to engender a spirit of international co-operation in a common constructive task. These considerations suggest that, however powerful countervailing factors may be, an element of international administration should enter into the proposed program.

Third, it would be desirable to set up the program in such a way as to remove it from the atmosphere of East-West competition. If, as may well be the case, the Soviets regard trade and aid as principal instruments of this competition, they will presumably not accept proposals which would remove some of the competitive elements. In any case it would be desirable in some way to face them with the choice. This could be done by offering them membership in the international programming body proposed below, and by thus providing a mechanism through which our assistance to the growth of viable, independent economies could be co-ordinated with whatever assistance they are willing to provide for the same purposes.

Fourth, whatever institutions are set up to execute the program, they should be in a position to apply reasonably strict criteria of economic productivity in meeting requests for funds. The need to apply fairly strict criteria suggests that some requests will have to be turned down. Should these refusals generate great ill will and suspicion that inappropriate criteria are being applied, two contrary dangers would emerge. One is that recipient countries might refuse to co-operate with the supplying organization, thereby frustrating the purposes of the program. The other danger is that the supplying institution, in order to avoid this consequence, might lower its standards to the point where it lost the respect and support of contributors. In either case the program would come to a halt. It is not at all clear that an international body is inherently any more or less likely to meet this condition than a national agency. While an international body may be less subject to specific national political interests, it will be more susceptible to appeals to relax criteria on alleged grounds of equity in distributing its resources among all its members. In the end, the possibility of applying firm criteria will depend much more on the sustained wisdom, judgment, and courage of the officials recruited to administer the program than on the national or international character of the administration.

This leads us to the fifth consideration, namely, that the amount of new and unfamiliar machinery should be kept to an absolute minimum. Where institutions already exist possessing trained and competent staffs which have over the years painfully acquired an understanding of elements of the problem, they should be utilized to the fullest extent possible. In particular we are impressed with the fact that the International Bank has built up a staff trained in the objective examination of economic development programs, is in a position to win the increasing respect of its members as an impartial and objective organization, and has built a reputation as a sound financial institution. Efforts should be made to find ways to use these assets more broadly in any enlarged effort. The shortage of trained and competent investigators and administrators is probably the most serious handicap which a program of this kind will have to overcome. The underdeveloped countries, having crying needs for such people in their own internal programs, simply cannot spare substantial

numbers of technicians to staff big new international sec-
retariats, and they should not be placed under pressure to
do so. Every proposed new organization chart must be
tested to see that the empty boxes on the diagram can
actually be filled with the names of first-rate people who
can be spared from whatever they are now doing. Many
schemes which look most attractive on other grounds will
fail this test.

The sixth consideration probably overrides all the others
in determining the institutional machinery best suited to
provide the additional funds which present sources are
unable to supply. This is that the principal supplying
nations must have sufficient confidence in whatever institutions are set up to supply them with adequate funds to do
the job on terms which will insure that it is done effectively. The proposal requires, above all, enough capital to
match absorptive capacity and it requires continuity. In
Chapter 10 we estimated that the additional rate of capital
flow to all the underdeveloped areas resulting from the
application of the criteria outlined in Chapter 7 might
reach from 2.5 to 3.5 billion dollars per year, if all underdeveloped countries were equally effective in boosting
their technical absorptive capacity. We guessed that perhaps a quarter of this could be supplied by the International
Bank, the International Finance Corporation, and private
sources, leaving 1.9 to 2.4 billion per year to be supplied
from all sources by grants and loans not bankable with
existing institutions. We further estimated that perhaps
no more than 60 per cent of this would actually be required

in any given year because many countries would not for some time take the action necessary to qualify under the criteria laid down. Even under the most conservative estimate of probable actual requirements, however, this program will call for financing through new institutions at a rate of well over a billion dollars a year. The U.S. share of this would have to be at least three quarters of a billion annually after the first two or three years. Is it realistic to hope that any United States Congress, even if it accepted the principles advocated in this book, would turn over nearly a billion dollars annually for administration and allocation by a new and untested international organization free of any U.S. control or accountability? It may be worth testing the realism of this hope; but we are skeptical.

As to continuity, we have reiterated our conviction that an assurance that the program would last on a substantial scale for at least five years is absolutely essential if the program is to have the desired effects. The proposers of the SUNFED plan were themselves so doubtful of the possibility of getting contributions on other than a year-to-year basis that they rejected the idea of proposing longer-term commitments for contributors. If the choice were between a series of national programs with a five-year horizon and an internationally administered program with no such assurance of continuity, we believe the bilateral alternative would be distinctly preferable, especially if the various national programs were co-ordinated by an international consultative agency.

A Compromise Conclusion

What do we conclude from this set of considerations as to the best machinery to handle the two new functions: of co-ordination, and of financing beyond the capabilities of existing sources? As to co-ordination, there is every reason why this should be handled by an international agency and no reason why it should not. In order to avoid the proliferation of unnecessary new machinery and to utilize existing skills, talents, and accumulated data, we believe this new agency should co-operate as closely as possible with the International Bank. It should, however, have a separate executive body and a Director General not involved in any of the Bank's lending activities. It could take over from the Bank some of its present functions of conducting country studies and reviewing over-all programs. It could have its own staff but should have the authority to utilize any of the staff and the material of the Bank in its information gathering and programming activities. Members who join—both suppliers and recipients— should commit themselves to supply full information on all their economic development activities, and to consult with the Agency before making or acting on applications for development assistance. Recipients should be prepared to discuss fully with the Agency their development programs and their plans to finance them, and suppliers should stand ready to consult, at the Agency's request, with other suppliers and with recipients on co-ordinated means of financing. The Agency would be charged with attempting to secure agreement among suppliers and between them and recipients on the criteria to be applied in acting on requests for assistance. The Agency should have as one of its functions the promotion of private capital movements. In addition to supplying information and arranging contacts between private investors and enterprises in need of funds, it might undertake the negotiation among all governments concerned of an international code governing the treatment of foreign capital invested in a country. It should report annually on the economic progress of the underdeveloped areas, and these reports should be of high intellectual quality, drafted independently of governments and political pressure.

Whether this Agency acquired respect, status, and influence would depend on the degree to which the major suppliers, especially the United States, and some of the leading recipients determined to use it and to make it a success. If new international financing institutions were not set up, this Agency would be the principal instrument for giving an international, multilateral character to economic development efforts. Since it is not proposed that it be given coercive powers or direct control over funds, its success, especially at first, would depend on the voluntary use made of it by its members. The history of the Colombo Plan demonstrates that where the members of a consultative organization of this kind have common objectives, it can be an effective instrument. If the United States, in particular, accepts the principles laid down in this book, there is no reason why such an Agency could not meet much of the need for multilateral machinery. If the United States is not ready for this kind of a program, it will surely not accept any alternative involving tighter international control.

As to financing, we are skeptical of the possibility of the SUNFED solution. Specifically, we doubt that the principal supplying nations would participate on the required scale. The SUNFED proposals involve a minimum fund of 250 million dollars. There has been a good deal of support for this proposal but also a good deal of vigorous opposition. We believe a program of this limited scale and without continuity would be a mistake. If it is simply to be one more piece of machinery additional to some new national (and especially U.S.) agencies, we do not think its symbolic advantages would compensate for the added complexity. If it is to be the only added effort, it will not be enough to get the underdeveloped countries across the threshold. Beyond this, an international agency with inadequate funds would be in grave danger of frittering away its limited resources in a large number of small grants designed to satisfy all its members that each would get a piece of the pie. If further exploration suggests that it is realistic to contemplate something at least four or five times this big, with commitments from suppliers for at least five years, further study of how it might be organized would be worth while. Pending such evidence, we are inclined to place reliance for internationalization of the program on the co-ordination and programming Agency suggested above, and to look essentially to national (or, perhaps, regional) bodies to supply the needed funds.

U.S. Action Required

In the light of this view, the United States should urgently undertake serious discussions with the governments of other supplying countries both as to the order of magnitude of the contribution they might be willing to make to a program of this kind and as to what institutions they might want to set up to handle their share of it. Some may prefer strictly national bodies. The Commonwealth countries might contemplate pooling their resources more fully than they have done under the Colombo Plan machinery. Western Europe might set up a financing instrument under the O.E.E.C. Provided all agreed to a reasonable consultative machinery such as proposed above, there is no reason why a variety of financing institutions could not work together, each meeting the institutional preferences of one or a group of supplying countries.

In the United States there should probably be a new agency. If it is to follow the quasi-banking principles proposed in Chapter 6, it should be separate from any of the regular Departments such as State and Defense. To achieve long-term continuity, it might be set up with a capital fund in the manner of the Export-Import Bank or the Reconstruction Finance Corporation, with a provision that up to a stated fraction of this fund could be used for activities from which no repayment was expected. As the fund was drawn upon, especially for grants, it could be replenished by annual Congressional appropriations, but these should be in the nature of contributions to capital expendable over at least a five-year period.

Technical assistance should continue to be handled partly through the United Nations and partly through national bodies in a better position than the U.N. to recruit certain kinds of people. In the U.S. technical assistance should likewise be set up with more assurance of continuity than in the past. Many kinds of technical assistance will be effective only if carried out over a period of five years or longer. To persuade high-caliber Americans to undertake assignments of this kind, there must be time for them to rearrange other commitments, assurance that they can finish the job once started, and some planning for what they will come back to when their technical assistance mission is completed. A quasi-autonomous body is needed to direct technical assistance. It might take the form of a special unit within the new American development authority suggested above, with financing which permitted the planning of technical assistance expenditures over a several-year period.

Serious thought should be given to devices which would make it possible for U.S. citizens to participate voluntarily in the financing of the new development authority. We believe there are many people in this country who, if given an opportunity, would like to invest part of their savings in programs to develop the underdeveloped areas. This opportunity might be offered through a small-denomination bond issue, guaranteed by the U.S. Treasury but separately identified as development bonds. Holders of such bonds would receive literature at regular intervals on the progress being made by the countries receiving capital from the development authority. There might even be ways of introducing equity features into such securities, the rate of return being dependent in some way on the behavior of an index of national output in borrowing countries. If such an issue carried reasonable terms from the investor's point of view, we believe the demand for it might be substantial; and it would permit American citizens to associate themselves individually with the constructive efforts going forward within the underdeveloped areas.

12 THE PROGRAM IN SUMMARY

THE PROPOSALS MADE IN THE foregoing chapters may be summarized as follows:

A. The United States should launch at the earliest possible moment a long-term program to promote sustained economic growth in the Free World. This program would make available to the underdeveloped countries sufficient additional capital and technical assistance to satisfy all likely demands for such assistance which meet fairly high standards of eligibility based on the prospective productivity of investment. The levels of investment assumed would be sufficient to make possible at least an over-all 1.5 or 2 per cent annual increase in real income per capita for all the underdeveloped countries of the Free World. In practice, some would grow faster, some slower than this rate.

B. As part of this program the U.S. government should

offer to provide a new long-term capital fund of from approximately ten to twelve billion dollars to be made available over a five-year period for loans and grants to accelerate economic growth in underdeveloped countries. In many instances individual loans and grants should be in the form of stand-by agreements covering the full period of a national development program. Although an initial five-year allocation is recommended, the plan would look ahead for a longer period, at least a decade.

C. This sum provided by the United States should be accompanied by commitments from the governments of other advanced industrialized countries to make additional loans and grants of from two to three billion dollars over the same time period as part of a unified Free World program.

D. Concerted measures should be taken to enlarge the international flows of private capital. Such measures might yield an addition over present levels of $2 to $2.5 billion during the first five-year period.

E. These sums must be made available to Free World countries without any military or political strings, but under strict businesslike criteria designed to guarantee that the loans and grants could be effectively used and that the loans could be repaid within a reasonable period of time.

F. Although it is most unlikely, if such criteria are enforced, that the whole of the sums offered would be taken up, it is essential that availability of the full amount be guaranteed in order to remove lack of capital as a bottleneck to economic growth and to provide maximum stimulus for the governments and peoples of the underdeveloped countries to expand their capacities to use capital effectively.

G. A systematic plan should be worked out for mobilizing stocks of agricultural surpluses to be made available for development purposes through an international food and fiber bank. Such a plan must insure that distribution of food and fiber stocks would not interfere with the normal markets of exporting countries.

H. Loans and grants should be administered by existing national and international agencies, including the Export-Import Bank, the International Bank, and the Colombo Plan organization; but new machinery must be created to co-ordinate information, set the ground rules, and secure acceptance of the criteria for the investment program.

I. If the U.S. capital made available under this program is to have its full potential effect in providing a lubricant to international trade, we must refrain from attaching "buy American" conditions on our contribution. In addition, if we are to persuade the underdeveloped countries and the other industrialized nations to move toward an increasing volume of trade and an effective international division of labor, we must take the lead by pursuing more vigorously the relaxation of our own barriers to international commerce.

We cannot emphasize too strongly that this program will not achieve its basically political and psychological purposes unless its fundamental features are preserved. Dilution could prove extremely dangerous. The sharp edges of policy which must be preserved appear to be these:

A. The additional sums envisaged must be large enough to remove lack of capital as a bottleneck to growth, while maintaining the tough criteria of productivity envisaged.

B. There must be no tie between economic aid and military pacts, and no explicit political conditions within the Free World beyond the requirement that national development goals be democratically established. An aid program with strings yields satellites, not partners.

C. The plan must look to a long future and envisage a sustained U.S. effort.

D. There must be a real measure of international contribution and international administration.

13 THE PROPOSAL IN THE SETTING OF NATIONAL POLICY

IT IS TIME, NOW, TO DRAW back from the details of our proposal and to examine how it relates to fundamental American interests; how it relates to the threats which confront the nation; how it could affect our relations with the Communist bloc. This appraisal requires a definition of the national interest and a characterization of the dangers we face.

What Is the National Interest?

The fundamental task of American military and foreign policy is to maintain a world environment for the United States within which our form of society can continue to develop in conformity with the humanistic principles which are its foundation. We must, of course, physically protect our own country; but the protection of American territory is essentially a means to a larger end—the protection of our still-developing way of life.

If the problem of national security is viewed in these terms—as the problem of protecting not merely the nation's real estate but also its basic values as a society—it follows that the United States has two distinct but connected interests in the vast continent of Eurasia. Since the combined resources of Eurasia could pose a serious threat of military defeat to the United States, it is our interest that no single power or group of powers, hostile or potentially hostile to the United States, dominate that area. Since, whatever the military situation might be, a Eurasia under totalitarian dictatorships would threaten the survival of democracy both elsewhere and in the United States, it is equally our interest that the societies of Eurasia develop along lines broadly consistent both with our own conception of the proper relation of the individual to the state and with their own cultural heritages.

We do not seek societies abroad built in our own image. We do have a profound interest that societies abroad develop and strengthen those elements in their respective cultures that elevate and protect the dignity of the individual as against the claims of the state. Such elements of harmony with the Western democratic tradition exist in different forms everywhere; and they have been strengthened by the attractiveness of the Western democratic example at its best, notably by the example of the American revolution and the values on which historically our society was erected and on which, by and large, it has subsequently operated.

We have, in short, a major and persistent stake in a world environment predominantly made up of open societies; for with modern communications it is difficult to envisage the survival of a democratic American society as an island in a totalitarian sea.

In terms of geography, it is a persistent interest of the United States that no single power or power grouping militarily dominate either Western or Eastern Eurasia. In Western Eurasia the threat of such an outcome is posed for us by the virtual absorption within the Soviet empire of East Germany and Eastern Europe. The threat would become virtually a reality should West Germany be lost to the Free World. In the East the threat of such an outcome is posed for us by the close alliance of the Soviet Union and Communist China. The situation in Asia is, however, more complicated than in Europe. Whereas in Europe West Germany, by and large, is the crux of the matter, in Asia there is Japan on the one hand and the whole area of Southeast Asia on the other, Southeast Asia stretching from Indo-China around Thailand, Burma, Malaya, Indonesia, India, and Pakistan. In Asia the threat would become virtually a reality should either Japan or Southeast Asia be lost to the Free World.

It is plain that the Communist world poses two threats to the United States—a military threat and an ideological threat. These threats are clearly related: the ideological loss of India, for instance, would raise important military problems; the military loss of northern Indo-China has raised important problems of ideological orientation throughout Southeast Asia. But the two American interests are not and should not be considered identical. The time necessary and the kind of effort required to cope with the military threat are likely to differ from those required by the ideological threat. The military threat to South Korea was dealt with in a few years; to defeat the ideological threat to South Korea may remain a creative Free World task for a generation.

If this view of the American interest is correct, the debate which has been proceeding in the United States over recent years as to whether the nation's interest should be defined in power terms or in terms of the ideological principles to which American society is attached is a somewhat misguided debate. This is so in two respects.

First, if the essential American interest is to preserve a world environment within which our form of democratic society can persist and develop, then the nation's stake in the ideological and political balance in Eurasia is as legitimate as its interest in the military balance of power in Eurasia. Two national efforts, one military and the other political, interacting intimately, must go forward together as part of a total effort to protect the interests of American society.

There is a second sense in which the debate appears misguided. It appears to be a characteristic of American history that this nation cannot be effective in its military and foreign policy unless it believes that both its security interests and its commitment to certain moral principles require the nation to act. From the Spanish-American War to the present the nation has acted effectively only when both strands in its interest were believed to be involved: in the Spanish-American War itself; in the First and Second World Wars; in the effort to reconstruct Western Europe, in 1947-1950; in the early phases of the Korean War. When idealism alone seemed to be the basis for the positions we have taken, the nation did not back its play; for example, in the open-door policy and in Wilson's ideological formulation of the American interests at Versailles. Equally, the nation has not been effective when it was confronted with situations where its power interests might be involved but where a persuasive moral basis for American action was not present. The notion of American imperialism, popular in certain American circles at the turn of the century, died quickly when it confronted the deep American instinct in support of political independence, as in the case of the Philippines and elsewhere. Similarly, a major reason why the United States was ineffective in the Indo-China crisis of 1954 was that it was then extremely difficult simultaneously to deal with the Communist menace and to disengage from French imperialism in that area.

In general, then, a sound American policy should be based upon a day-to-day awareness of the military and nonmilitary actions required to defend and perpetuate the quality of our society as well as to maintain its physical security, and upon an awareness of the American need to believe that both interests and ideals are at stake, before sustained and effective public support can be evoked. The art of American statesmanship is to formulate courses of action which in specific settings harmonize abiding American interests and abiding American ideals.

The Threats to the American Interest

In the light of this conception of the American interest it is possible to define in reasonable order the threats which the nation now faces. The American interest is threatened by three potential forms of Communist military aggression. It is also urgently and immediately threatened by the psychological, economic, and political offensive now being conducted from Moscow and Peking and designed to disengage the United States from power and influence in the Eurasian continent. The military and nonmilitary aspects of Communist policy are closely linked. In addition to these immediate military and nonmilitary threats, the American interest faces a long-run danger of isolation from Eurasia, quite independent of current Communist activities and independent, even, of the existence of a world-wide Communist movement. This whole spectrum of threats can be defined as follows.

The Three Military Threats

The most obvious danger the United States confronts is that the Soviet Union may acquire in the technological arms race a lead sufficient for the men in Moscow rationally to envisage a sudden attack designed to eliminate American retaliatory power at a blow. The achievement of such a decisive lead is by no means easy in the modern world; and it should not be identified with a lead in one form of delivery technique—for example, the possible current Soviet edge in medium range and intercontinental guided or ballistic missiles. It is possible for one power to have a very substantial lead over the other and still find it irrational to envisage an all-out attack because it could not count on sufficient destruction of the other's retaliatory power to avoid grievous if not decisive damage being done to its own society. Nevertheless, notably in the case of long-range missiles, it is evident that the first charge on American security policy is to avoid any possibility of being so outstripped technologically by the Soviet Union as to be vulnerable to the wiping out of the American retaliatory force in a single wave of attack.

While the danger of a successful Soviet aerial blitzkrieg is real but not imminent, the erosion of the American military position in Eurasia, because of Soviet equality or superiority in weapons of mass destruction, is already under way. The Soviets have succeeded over the past decade in rapidly closing the gap in weapons of mass destruction, in the means of their delivery, and in the means of defense against them. They have used this developing capability to support, in effect, a program of political blackmail. By means which are either subtle or unsubtle, as occasion demands, Moscow is telling American allies and potential allies that American military strength can no longer protect them; that should major war come, the United States could not prevent their national destruction with Soviet weapons. Therefore, Moscow argues, the only rational course for other countries is to disengage from alliances with the United States, an argument of some evident persuasiveness from Iceland to Ceylon. This policy of blackmail almost certainly could not be effective if conducted in Stalin's inimitable style; by and large, when men are sufficiently frightened they cling together and exhibit considerable courage in the face of the raw threat of force. The present Soviet leadership, however, has conducted its policy of threat with some subtlety. It has gained considerable force from the fact that it is accompanied by a psychological, political, and economic policy that is designed not merely to make association with the United States unattractive but also to make association with Moscow more attractive. Soviet policy is now an extremely effective mixture of stick and carrot; and it threatens to break up the American military alliances in Eurasia and to disengage us from some of our major overseas bases.

The third military threat is that of limited war conducted under circumstances in which the United States finds it impossible to bring into play the major instruments in being of its military strength; that is, American air and naval power, applying atomic weapons. By and large, Moscow and Peking have behaved since the summer of 1951 as though they regarded limited war as an unsatisfactory instrument for expanding Communist influence and authority. Nevertheless, in Asia, the Middle East, and Africa the Free World is vulnerable to degrees of military aggression along the lines of the Free World's experience in Greece, Berlin, Malaya, Indo-China, and (least likely) Korea. The degree of vulnerability to limited war depends in substantial part on the political, social, and economic soundness of various Free World areas, since the effective use of Communist techniques of limited war hinges on the infiltration of weak, divided societies and consequent internal disintegration. In the revolutionary transitions through which many societies in the Free World are now passing we can mitigate periods of weakness and division by our nonmilitary policy, but we cannot guarantee that they will not occur. We cannot, therefore, rule out the possibility of having to face "brushfire" wars.

These problems may assume two distinct forms corresponding to two different possible Communist strategies. One now familiar form of outbreak arises where external Communist support is given a local insurrectional group within which Communist leadership is predominant. We have confronted this kind of problem, for example, in Greece, the Philippines, and Indo-China. In such situations the Communists hope that, by backing militarily a faction over which they have substantial control, they can directly gain control over a disputed area.

A second form of outbreak may be more probable in the future. It is a cardinal principle of Communist doctrine that in areas where an immediate seizure of power by a Communist party is not possible their long-run interest is best served by weakening "bourgeois" governments in any ways that present themselves. Outside Communist-dominated areas their purposes are served by encouraging chaos and conflict. This is the kind of problem faced potentially in the Middle East, in Kashmir, and in parts of Africa. It is an evident interest of Moscow to promote such disruptive schisms in the Free World by raising the level of tension, sometimes by egging on both parties to a conflict, even though there are in prospect no immediate gains for local Communists. The American interest, on the other hand, is opposed to the heightening of tensions anywhere, since the long-run constructive forces which we believe will assert themselves if given a chance cannot operate in crisis situations. Men who are close to violence cannot direct their full energies to building stable, effective societies. American nonmilitary as well as military policy must be designed to cope with this second type of brush-fire as well as with the first.

The Urgent Nonmilitary Threat

The most evident and urgent threat to the American interest now consists in the psychological, political, and economic policy by which Moscow and Peking seek progressively to eliminate the United States from influence and power in Eurasia, and, in appropriate stages, to draw the nations of Western Europe, the Middle East, Africa, and Asia into the orbit of communism. Moscow's method is to associate itself ostensibly with the aspirations of the people of the Free World for peace, economic progress, and political independence. This policy has been under way since, roughly, the summer of 1951. It was articulated by

Stalin at the Nineteenth Congress of the Communist Party in 1952; it was developed with great vigor and tactical imagination after Stalin's death; and it has been notably reinforced by the dramatic, symbolic acts of the Twentieth Party Congress in 1956, notably the theological demotion of Stalin and the elevation of Lenin to unique ideological stature.

The political, economic, and psychological elements in the present Soviet and Chinese Communist offensive are being adapted with skill to the problems and possibilities of different areas in the Free World. In France and Italy the principal emphasis is on the building of popular-front governments and creating an environment in which they are likely to thrive. In Germany the bait of German unity is being steadily held out in return for a rupture of the NATO tie. In Britain and Japan as well as in Western Germany the possibilities of trade with the Communist bloc are held forth. In the Middle East the association with unsatisfied national aspirations is linked with credits, technical assistance, and trade in products difficult to market within the Free World under current circumstances. In Southeast Asia the objective is to use every economic, political, and psychological device to encourage neutralism wherever it exists and to create the foundations for the development of local communism on a popular-front basis.

In the context of American policy over the past five years the Soviet offensive is formidably effective. It not only threatens to undermine politically American military alliances and the American base structure, but it also threatens to reduce progressively the political influence of the United States in Eurasia and to open the way for later degenerative processes that might make possible actual Communist take-over.

A Longer-Run Danger to the American Interest

In the opening of this chapter the American interest was defined in terms which include but transcend the problem of countering Communist aggressive objectives and techniques. The American interest has been rather considered to be the maintenance of a military and political environment in Eurasia such that American society can continue to develop along lines consonant with the nation's basic historic values. At the moment the spectrum of threats which confront the nation stems from a systematic exploitation by Moscow and Peking of certain conditions within the Free World. When one looks ahead over the next fifty to one hundred years, however, it seems altogether possible that the United States could be confronted with a major danger even if communism should wither away as an effective international force. The danger is that the underdeveloped countries develop along lines hostile to the West and Western tradition. The peoples of these countries constitute a very high proportion of the world's population. Should their basic orientation be anti-Western and anti-American, the United States would confront a very grave set of problems as the presently underdeveloped societies were modernized and strengthened. And such an evolution is not at all impossible. The colonial heritage of these regions, their powerful latent sense of hostility due to the problem of color, the difficulties through which they will have to pass if they are to gain modern status for their societies—all might well lead to attitudes of fixed and dangerous hostility which could eventually split the world on new lines. It is an American interest from the present forward so to associate ourselves with the evolution of the underdeveloped countries as to maximize the possibility that when they emerge to modern status the lines of association rather than of conflict between the United States and these areas are dominant. Their aspiration for the values of individual dignity, national independence, and material welfare make the triumph of these more hopeful strands by no means impossible.

The Role of the Proposed Program

The proposal made in this book emerges, then, as a substantial portion of a total policy designed to protect the nation's interest against the threats which confront us both in the immediate future and, foreseeably, over the longer term.

Our proposal is, of course, no substitute for a well-designed military policy although it is an indispensable element in a policy designed to minimize the possibilities of limited war in the underdeveloped areas. And, as the arms race in major weapons moves into what may be a protracted stalemate, this kind of war is the form of military engagement we are most likely to confront.

Our proposal is a positive answer to the immediate threat posed for us by the current political, economic, and psychological offensive of the Communist bloc.

Over the long pull, it is the most promising instrument we can devise to assure that the industrialized and underdeveloped areas ultimately emerge from the present revolutionary phase of history as members of a common, harmonious world community, dedicated to the proposition that the state is the servant of the individual.

Relations with the Communist Bloc

How might a proposal of this kind affect our relations with Moscow?

Its first and fundamental consequence would be to place the current Communist offensive in the underdeveloped countries in perspective and reduce its effectiveness and its danger to the Free World. The Communist offensive is clearly opportunist in character and disruptive in intent, and has gathered strength mainly because there has been a vacuum in American and Western policy in those countries. It is a firmly established fact that a number of leaders in the underdeveloped countries, having taken the measure of Moscow's intentions, are anxious to rebuild their relations with the United States and the West on some such basis as that proposed here.

With a gap in American and Western policy as real as the gap in our defenses in Korea in June, 1950, the current Communist offensive has had important effects.

Against the background of an American-initiated program of the kind proposed in this book, it would be vastly less impressive.

The United States and other nations of the Free World generally might then examine their economic relations to the Communist bloc in a new setting of poise and confidence.

Specifically, two questions arise: (1) What position should we take with respect to participation in the program by Communist bloc countries? (2) How might our policy with respect to East-West trade be affected by the plan?

Communist countries might participate in two ways. The Soviet Union itself could supply some capital for development, while some of its satellites, particularly China, might be potential recipients of loans. Our calculations of capital requirements and possible sources of supply have all been made on the probably reasonable assumption that the entire Communist bloc would remain outside the program, both as lenders and as borrowers. Consideration should nevertheless be given to whether Communist countries should not be invited to participate on the same terms as everyone else. No particular problems would seem to be raised by inviting contributions from Russia, so long as Moscow would agree to the kinds of criteria which the Free World would regard as acceptable, and so long as the question of Soviet participation was not permitted to slow down the development and execution of the scheme. If Moscow is invited to participate in order to remove the "economic competition" from the cold war, it must evidently be on the basis of no veto power in the international development body. On this condition there would seem to be every reason to make the invitation. If it is accepted, much of the political advantage Moscow has secured from the competition would disappear. If it is rejected, it will be a clear signal to the world that the Soviet Union wishes to use aid as a bilateral political tool. With a major, sustained Western initiative under way, based on positive principles, we could afford to let Moscow contribute as it would to the development of the Free World. There is no need for a purposeful, active Free World, grappling with its common problems on the scale those problems require, to take fright at the presence of a handful of Soviet technicians or even at Soviet credits and trade.

As to the satellites, some of the Eastern European states could qualify only as contributors; a few (probably Bulgaria, Rumania, and Albania) might qualify as borrowers, in addition to Communist China. The criterion that potential borrowers must submit detailed economic plans for international inspection and approval would, however, almost certainly exclude them in practice. The desirability of making the gesture would have to be determined by weighing the possible dangers of such a move against the not inconsiderable virtues of being able to announce that the plan is open to every country in the world which is willing to abide by the wholly nonpolitical conditions set upon participation.

For Moscow, of course, the proposed program would create an acute dilemma. The present Soviet policy in underdeveloped countries is based on a failure of the United States to associate itself positively with the constructive aspirations of the peoples in these areas. If the proposed program were successfully launched, Moscow would face the hard choice of joining it as a junior member, under circumstances likely to advance Free World interests, or of proceeding on its present bilateral course under unpromising circumstances, so far as Soviet purposes are concerned.

With respect to East-West trade we believe that this plan, if put into operation, might render this issue a less divisive one in the Free World than it is at present. Important groups in Europe and Asia have seen in an expansion of East-West trade one solution to the international economic problems of their countries, and have therefore strongly opposed our policy of restricting such trade.

It is our view that their hopes of a real solution in trade with the Communist bloc are mainly illusory. The economic position within the bloc, combined with its political policies, makes it, in fact, most unlikely that any substantial increase in East-West trade would take place if all controls by the West were dropped. It is certain, for example, that Communist China could not supply the commodities needed by Japan, on the requisite scale, without dismantling its trade ties with the Communist bloc—an outcome which is not in sight. Recent Soviet purchases of rice from Burma and cotton from Egypt have suggested dangers from the emergence of the Communist bloc as a major buyer of agricultural surpluses. If the selling countries can sell their surpluses to no one else and can secure capital for development in no other way, this is indeed a disturbing phenomenon. But if the West provides alternatives, we do not have to be concerned about the Soviet lure.

Our allies, both the developed countries like Germany, Britain, and Japan and the underdeveloped countries like Burma and Egypt, will tend to be attracted by dangling offers of East-West trade so long as they feel the pinch of inadequate Free World markets and inadequate supplies of nondollar foodstuffs and raw materials. Moscow and Peking can be relied upon to exploit this sense of marginal strain so long as it exists. The proposals set forth in this book would, in our judgment, permit a solid Free World solution without enlarged East-West trade, leaving the Free World to take or leave trade with the Communist bloc as it suited Free World interests.

Politically, East-West trade is neutral. Depending on the posture of the two trading partners, it can pull just as well on the East as on the West; or it may not pull either way. The basic rule of the West should be: the only safe East-West trade is that trade we are prepared to redirect on short notice. This requires, in general, a viable growing Free World economy of the kind envisaged in these proposals. It may require, in addition, special stockpiling provisions designed to permit a quick transfer of source of supply, for those commodities coming from the Communist bloc.

Against such a background the Free World would be able to play the game of East-West trade on a take-it-or-leave-it basis.

Generally speaking, then, the proposal presented here should remove the dangers arising from the blandishments of Communist economic foreign policy and permit the Free World to proceed with its business, with or without Communist participation and East-West trade, from a position of poise and confidence.

14 THE AMERICAN MISSION

IN ITS ESSENCE, OUR
proposal calls for a sustained effort by the United States
to associate its purposes and efforts with those of the aspir-
ing new nations. Quite aside from its virtue as a means of
protecting the national interest, this association could have
profound and wholesome effects on the quality of our
domestic life.

The United States is now within sight of solutions to the
range of issues which have dominated its political life since
1865. Our central problem has been to reconcile the
fact of industrialization with the abiding principles of
democracy. The farm problem, the status of big business in
a democratic society, the status and responsibilities of organized labor, the avoidance of extreme cyclical unemployment, social equity for the Negro, the provision of equal
educational opportunity, the equitable distribution of in-

come—none of all these great issues is fully resolved; but a national consensus on them exists within which we are clearly moving forward as a nation. The achievement of this consensus absorbed much of the nation's creativeness and idealism over the past ninety years. If we continue to devote our attention in the same proportion to domestic issues as in the past, we run the danger of becoming a bore to ourselves and the world. We shall be quarreling over increasingly smaller margins, increasingly narrower issues. While enjoying the material fruits of a rich and complacent society, we shall become progressively isolated from the vital issues of the world.

Our proposal requires that the United States allocate increased resources for loans, technical assistance, and some grants to other nations. The order of magnitude of these increased outlays is modest. Our annual gross national product is of the order of 400 billion dollars, and it should regularly increase each year by about 12 billion dollars. There is no question here of sacrificing our standard of living or of disrupting the workings of our economy. We can obviously afford to do the job. What is required to launch and execute this proposal is will, understanding, and a positive sense of our national purpose on the world scene.

From the revolutionary beginnings of our history the United States has, on balance, acted in loyalty to the conception that its society has a meaning and a purpose which transcend the nation. Down to the present day the peoples of the United States and of the world have not wholly lost the sense that this nation represents a continuing, unique experiment in the development of free societies. If over the coming decades the United States should turn its back on the great revolutionary transformations going forward in the underdeveloped countries, devoting itself almost exclusively to domestic chores and objectives, American society will progressively lose some of those basic spiritual qualities which have been historically linked to the nation's sense of world mission. The nation will risk the long-run danger of helping bring about, by its own spiritual decline, a kind of self-enforced isolation which would further damage the military and nonmilitary bases of national security.

On the other hand, the execution of the proposals presented in this book requires an active rededication to the fundamental principles which have given American life its distinction, its transcendent quality. The nation will have to sustain association with other nations over many years, bringing to bear its taxes and its talent, its sympathy, curiosity, and understanding. It will have to learn much of other peoples and come to know problems which the United States has long since outgrown or which it never faced.

All of this is to the good, for America at its best has never wholly lost a sense of the community of human destiny:

One thought ever at the fore—
That in the Divine Ship, the World, breasting Time and
  Space,
All peoples of the globe together sail, sail the same voyage,
Are bound to the same destination.

APPENDIX

The Estimation of Capital Requirements for Development

Statistical information on the economies of the underdeveloped countries is of very varying quality. Population data are in general the most reliable, national income estimates very much less so, and information on capital formation either nonexistent or very incomplete. The figures on which the calculations which follow are based are thus a combination of official data which we have adjusted where possible to make them comparable and rough estimates based on guesses which we hope are intelligent. We believe they give a roughly correct indication of orders of magnitude, but any of them may be in error by as much as 20 or 25 per cent.

Our procedure as indicated in Chapter 10 has been first to estimate the national incomes of the underdeveloped countries by regions in U.S. dollars for the year 1953. Second, we have made estimates of gross capital formation for the same year. Third, we have adjusted these to a net basis by making an allowance—usually a pure guess—for capital expenditures required to maintain existing capital intact. Fourth, we have made an estimate for each region of the upper limit of the additional outside capital we think might in a peak year be called for in each region if all countries were efficient in meeting the criteria discussed in Chapter 7. Fifth, we have applied an assumed ratio of new capital invested to additional output produced in order to derive the annual rate of growth of national income which might result from the estimated level of capital formation. Sixth, we have listed the population of each region as given in U.N. publications. Seventh, we have estimated the annual rate of population increase of each region. Finally, eighth, we have subtracted the rate of population increase from the rate of increase of income to get a possible annual rate of increase of per capita income. The resulting figures are given in Table 1.

The following comments explain sources and assumptions used in each line of the table:

1. The national income estimates are taken from "Estimate of World Income, 1953" by Melville H. Watkins, prepared at the Center for International Studies, Massachusetts Institute of Technology, Cambridge, Massachusetts. These estimates are based upon United Nations figures where available, converted to dollars at the prevailing exchange rate, where a representative rate could be found. Where U.N. data were not available, where there was evidence that the 1953 exchange rate was markedly unrepresentative of the foreign exchange purchasing power of the currency, or where no meaningful exchange rate could be found, other methods of estimation were used. These are explained in the source document, available from the Center.

2. The data on gross capital formation in local currency are largely drawn from United Nations Statistical Papers, Series H, No. 8, and have been converted into U.S. dollars at the effective conversion ratios used in "Estimate of World Income,

TABLE 1

POSSIBLE CAPITAL FORMATION AND INCOME GROWTH IN THE UNDERDEVELOPED COUNTRIES BY REGIONS

	South Central Asia	Rest of Asia	Middle East	Latin America	Africa	Total
National Income—$ Billion—1953	27.9	19.7	12.3	40.4	10.1	110.4
Gross Capital Formation—$ Billion—1953	2.8	1.7	1.5	7.1	1.2	14.3
Net Capital Formation—$ Billion—1953	1.7	1.2	0.9	4.3	0.7	8.2
Upper Limit of Proposed Annual Additional Capital Inflow	1.0	0.6	0.5	1.0	0.4	3.5
% Annual Income Increase	3.3	3.0	3.8	4.37	3.6	
Population (millions)—1953	459	231	90	173	173	1,126
% Annual Population Increase	1.3	1.6	1.8	2.25	1.5	
% Annual Per Capita Income Increase	2.0	1.4	2.0	2.12	2.1	

The regional grouping used in the above table is as follows:

South Central Asia: India, Pakistan, and Ceylon

Rest of Asia: the balance of non-Communist Asia excluding the Middle East and Japan, i.e., Afghanistan, Burma, Cambodia, Formosa, Hong Kong, Indonesia, Laos, Nepal, South Korea, Malaya and Singapore, Philippines, Thailand, Vietnam, and the Pacific Islands.

Middle East: the Arabian Peninsula, Cyprus, Egypt, Iran, Iraq, Israel, Jordan, Lebanon, Syria, Turkey, and the Persian Gulf states

Latin America: all the countries of South and Central America

Africa: all the countries of the African continent except Egypt and the Union of South Africa

1953." For the numerous countries for which no data was available, the estimates are guesses based on what seemed to be reasonable assumptions.

3. The deductions for investment required to maintain capital intact are in some cases based on reported depreciation figures, but for the most part depend on some very general assumptions.

4. For the rest of Asia, the Middle East, and Africa, the upper limit of proposed annual additional capital inflow has been taken as 35 per cent of gross capital formation for 1953, rounded off to the nearest hundred million dollars. For Latin America the figure used was 14 per cent on the ground that several of the principal Latin American countries are emerging into the third stage of growth in which their requirements for foreign capital from other than normal sources are declining.

5. The annual rates of increase in income were calculated by applying a capital-output ratio of 3:1 to the sum of net capital investment in 1953 plus the upper limit of proposed additional capital inflow (rows 3÷4). For particular countries the capital-output ratio may be even lower than 3:1, in which case the rates of increase of income will be correspondingly higher.

6. The population figures are drawn from the United Nations *Demographic Yearbook*, 1954.

7. The rates of population increase have been estimated with the assistance of "Framework for Future Population Estimates, 1950–1980, by World Regions," prepared by John D. Durand

for the 1954 World Population Conference at Rome (mimeo.).

With one exception, the estimates, while subject to very large margins of error, are designed to be our best guesses as to the relevant magnitudes. It should be emphasized that the estimate of proposed additional capital inflow is designed as an estimate of an upper limit set by absorptive capacity on the assumption that all countries will be vigorous in expanding their capacity to absorb capital as rapidly as possible. The flow in any one year under the program proposed in this book will be substantially less for two reasons. First, absorptive capacity will undoubtedly not be pressed to these upper limits by some countries. Second, the speed with which different countries will be able to react to the opportunity offered by this program will vary greatly from country to country depending on each country's stage of development. A few will have large requirements in the near future. As time passes, they will become increasingly capable of meeting their own requirements from their own growing output as others reach the point where their needs and capacities to use foreign capital are growing.

To illustrate how a country once launched on the growth process with the aid of capital from abroad is ultimately able to generate its own capital requirements for growth, we have constructed a number of growth models based on arbitrary assumptions. For example, if the initial rate of domestic investment in a country is 5 per cent of national income, if foreign capital is supplied at a constant rate equal to one-third the initial level of domestic investment, if 25 per cent of all additions to income are saved and reinvested, if the capital-output ratio is 3, and if interest and transferred dividend service on foreign loans and private investments are paid at the rate of 6 per cent per year, the country will be able to discontinue net foreign borrowing after fourteen years and sustain a 3 per cent rate of growth of income out of its own resources. The period required to reach self-sustaining growth will, of course, be longer if the initial rate of saving or the marginal rate of saving is lower, if the capital-output ratio is higher, or if the interest and amortization charges are higher, and vice versa.

It would be convenient if we could present, for comparative purposes, a picture of how much of the capital formation in each region in 1953 was supplied from abroad. Unfortunately the data do not permit this. The following tables contain information on capital supplied to the underdeveloped areas from a number of sources.

TABLE 2

SUMMARY ESTIMATE OF FOREIGN SOURCES OF CAPITAL FOR UNDER-DEVELOPED COUNTRIES

(In Millions of U.S. Dollars)

	1953	Five-Year Average*
U.S. direct investment in underdeveloped areas abroad: Net capital outflow including undistributed earnings of subsidiaries	570¶	533¶
Investment income	(1,007)	(1,018)
U.S. Government foreign economic grants	623	
Export-Import Bank: Disbursements	433†	436‡
Repayments	−65	
I.B.R.D. Disbursements§	112	114
European foreign private investment and public investment in overseas territories	1,275	
Total (rounded)		$3.0 billion

* Roughly the period covered is 1951–1955 inclusive, but the figures do not all refer to exactly the same calendar period.

¶ From this should be deducted amortization service on foreign bonds in U.S. which amounts to slightly under $100 million.

† Includes $300 million balance of payments credit to Brazil.

‡ A breakdown of loans from July 1, 1950, to December 31, 1954, shows approximately one-third were project credits, i.e., loans which made a direct contribution to economic development.

§ Repayments are not significant.

TABLE 3

U.S. DIRECT INVESTMENT ABROAD BY REGIONS, 1953

(In Millions of U.S. Dollars)

	Net Capital Outflow	Less Transferred Income	Net
Latin America	288	583	−295
South Central Asia (India)	6	9	−3
' Rest of Asia (Indonesia & Philippines)	24	56	−32
Middle East (Israel)	14	—	14
Africa	57	25	32
Western European dependencies (excepting Western Hemisphere & Africa)	102	101	1
Other underdeveloped countries	79	233	−154
Total underdeveloped countries	570	1,007	−437
World Totals	1,497	1,398	99

FIVE-YEAR AVERAGE (1950–1954 INCLUSIVE)
(In Millions of U.S. Dollars)

	Net Capital Outflow	Less Transferred Income	Net
Latin America	342	588	−246
South Central Asia (India)	13	11	2
Rest of Asia (Indonesia & Philippines)	18	54	−36
Middle East (Israel)	13	1	12
Africa	53	34	19
Western European dependencies (excepting Western Hemisphere & Africa)	19	93	−74
Other underdeveloped countries	75	237	−162
Total underdeveloped countries	533	1,018	−485
World Totals	1,410	1,454	−44

NOTES

1. The classification is as contained in the source: *Survey of Current Business*, August, 1955. It would appear that oil-producing countries of the Middle East are included under "Other countries" and "Western European dependencies." The U.N. publication "Economic Development in the Middle East, 1945–54" shows U.S. direct investment 1944–53 as $824 million, of which 90 per cent is petroleum and most of the balance manufactures in Israel.

2. Net Capital Outflow includes the undistributed earnings of subsidiaries. Income is the sum of dividends, interest, and

branch profits. The following is a breakdown of undistributed earnings of subsidiaries for 1953:

Latin America	166
South Central Asia (India)	3
Rest of Asia	5
Middle East (Israel)	1
Africa	46
Western European dependencies (excepting Western Hemisphere and Africa)	22
Other countries	45
Total	288

TABLE 4

U.S. FOREIGN ECONOMIC GRANTS, 1953

U.S. Government Foreign Grants, Economic and Relief:
Net Utilized

(In Millions of U.S. Dollars)

Latin America	23
South Central Asia (India and Pakistan)	117
Rest of Asia	353
Middle East	108
Africa	5
Other Asia*	8
Unspecified Asia*	9
Total	623

OTHER

Western Europe	1,160
Other Europe	8
International Organizations	36
Unspecified	14
Total	1,841

* Covers South Central Asia, Rest of Asia, Middle East (excluding Egypt and Turkey), and Japan.

The figures are those listed as "Economic and Relief" in Table B-3 of "Report of Activities of the National Advisory Council on International Monetary and Financial Problems," October 1, 1953, to June 30, 1954, and July to December 31, 1954. Only an undeterminable portion of these sums should properly be classified as capital for economic development. The balance is relief and assistance to the current budgets of allies maintaining large military establishments, principally Korea, Vietnam, and Formosa.

TABLE 5

CUMULATIVE U.S. AID EXPENDITURES, APRIL 3, 1948, TO JUNE 30, 1955

(In Millions of U.S. Dollars)

	Direct Forces Support	Defense Support	Development Assistance	Technical Co-operation	Other	Total
Latin America	—	—	8.9	65.7	—	74.6
South Central Asia	—	32.6	37.2	102.6	4.6	177.0
Rest of Asia	664.2	1,046.7	3.4	8.4	—	1,722.7
Middle East	15.8	315.5	336.2	93.0	—	760.5
Africa	—	—	7.9	18.6	—	26.5
Total	680.0	1,394.8	393.6	2,883.0	4.6	2,761.3
World Totals*	821.2	16,362.0	394.3	294.9	186.2	18,058.6

* Includes the following items which are applicable, at best in part, to the underdeveloped countries but cannot be fitted with our classifications.

Far East Program—Regional	1.5
Undistributed	8.8
Near East, Africa and South Asia Program—Regional	4.0
Undistributed	3.7
Nonregional	177.3

Source: ICA *Operations Report*, November 16, 1955. Although classifications of aid have been subject to some change over the period, it is believed that most of the above falls in the category of "Economic and Relief."

TABLE 6

U.S. GOVERNMENT FOREIGN CREDITS UTILIZED, 1953

(In Millions of U.S. Dollars)

	Export-Import Bank	Mutual Security	Lend-Lease & Other	Total
Latin America	398*	—	2	400
South Central Asia	—	8	—	8
Rest of Asia	22	1	—	23
Middle East (Israel & Turkey)	13	—	—	13
Africa	—	4	3	7
Totals	433	13	5	451
World Totals	647	54	8	709

* Includes $300 million balance-of-payments credit.

These figures represent utilization of U.S. Government foreign credits as shown in Table 8-9 of "Report of Activities of the National Advisory Council . . ."

EXPORT-IMPORT BANK—REPAYMENTS, 1953

(In Millions of U.S. Dollars)

Latin America	48
South Central Asia	—
Middle East	13
Africa	4
Total	65
World Total	310

Export-Import Bank—Net Credits
Authorized
Five-Year Average (July 1, 1950, to June 30, 1955)
(In Millions of U.S. Dollars)

Latin America	209.7
South Central Asia	—
Rest of Asia	9.6
Middle East	19.9
Africa	7.7
Total	246.9
World Total	435.7

Export-Import Bank—Classification of Net Credits Authorized July 1, 1950, to December 31, 1954.[*]
(In Millions of U.S. Dollars)

	Project Credits	Commodity Purchases	Strategic Materials	Other	Total
Latin America	409.4	25.9	119.8	326.0	881.1
South Central Asia	—	—	—	—	—
Rest of Asia	43.5	—	—	1.0	44.5
Middle East	92.8	—	—	—	92.8
Africa	23.4	—	—	—	23.4
Totals	569.1	25.9	119.8	327.0	1,041.8
World Totals	590.2	351.5	275.3	623.4	1,840.4

[*] Comparable breakdown for first six months of 1955 could not be located.

TABLE 7

INTERNATIONAL BANK FOR RECONSTRUCTION AND DEVELOPMENT DISBURSEMENTS
(In Millions of U.S. Dollars)

	To Underdeveloped Areas	Total
1951	73.9	128.9
1952	117.8	225.7
1953	112.1	239.8
1954	125.7	298.1
1955	142.3	284.5
Average	114.3	235.4

I.B.R.D. DISBURSEMENTS BY REGIONS
(In Millions of U.S. Dollars)

	1953	Five-Year Average
Latin America	49.9	63.7
South Central Asia	8.4	13.0
Rest of Asia	8.2	4.8
Middle East	10.7	9.7
Africa	34.9	23.1
Totals	112.1	114.3

Source: International Monetary Fund, *International Financial Statistics.*

Rough Estimates of Other Sources for Average Year
(In Millions of U.S. Dollars)

Private	U.K	200	
	France	200	
	Belgium	100	500
Public	U.K.	175*	
	France	600	775
			1,275

* Based on total expenditures under Colonial Welfare and Development but excluding sterling balances.

Other Sources

The total outflow of private long-term capital from other than the United States, for 1946–1952, has been estimated by the U.N. as $2.6 billion U.S. or approximately $400 million per annum. This can be broken down approximately as follows:

United Kingdom	1.2
France	1.0
Switzerland	0.4
Total	2.6

It is suggested that Belgium and the Netherlands are also net exporters on private long-term capital account.

The U.K. outflow can be further broken down in approximate U.S. million $ amounts as:

Government and municipal loans	400
Share and loan capital of registered companies	875
Direct investment	2,500
Total	1,225

A breakdown by countries or regions is available only for government and municipal loans and share and loan capital. The portion applicable to underdeveloped areas can largely be isolated.

Over the period 1946-1952, the interest and dividends paid on account of U.K. investments in companies operating abroad amounted to about $2,200 million.

Latin America	1,125
South Central Asia	30
Rest of Asia	15
Africa	100
Total	1,270

The figure for direct investment is a rough U.N. estimate, and no breakdown is available. It is believed that a considerable portion is accounted for by manufacturing in the United States, Australia, and the Union of South Africa, and that overseas petroleum investment presumably in the Middle East exceeded $600 million U.S. in this period. Data available for 1950–1954 suggest direct investment during this period of approximately $100 million U.S. in the Federation of Rhodesia and Nyasaland.

Little information is available to support the estimate for France. The balance of payments for the metropolitan franc area records a net inflow of capital of $330 million U.S. for the period 1946–1951, largely representing liquidation of

French long-term investments abroad. A regional breakdown of the balance of payments for 1951 shows most of the net inflow for that year as pertaining to the IMF classifications "United States and Canada" and "Continental OEEC." This suggests a gross outflow of approximately $1.3 billion U.S. for the period, mostly applicable to underdeveloped areas. The U.N. shows French private investment in her African colonies of approximately $275 million U.S. in 1953, and this suggests that a large portion of the gross outflow over the whole period is applicable to French Africa.

For Switzerland, of the $0.4 billion U.S. over the whole period, approximately $30 million U.S. is directly applicable to underdeveloped areas, and all went to the Belgian Congo. No statistics are available on direct investments, but they are known to have been active.

For Belgium, the principal outflow has been directed toward the Belgian Congo. New private investments in the Belgian Congo during the period 1945–1949 have been estimated at $300 million and during the four years 1948–1951 at about $400 million, mostly raised in Belgium or obtained through reinvestment of profits by Belgian companies in the Congo.

Public Investment

Expenditures by the U.K. government under the Colonial Welfare and Development Act were £s. 527 million for the period 1945–1955, and approximately £85 million is estimated to be applicable to development and welfare. The portion flowing to Africa has been fairly constant at £6 million annually.

French public investment in 1953 is estimated as $430 million to French North Africa and $175 million to French territories south of the Sahara.

Set in Linotype Fairfield
Format by Stephen King
Manufactured by The Haddon Craftsmen, Inc.
Published by HARPER & BROTHERS, New York